365
Fun Facts
for Catholic
Kids

Bernadette McCarver Snyder

Liguori

LIGUORI, MISSOURI

Published by Liguori Publications
Liguori, Missouri
www.liguori.org
www.catholicbooksonline.com

Imprimi Potest:
William A. Nugent, C.SS.R.
Provincial, St. Louis Province
The Redemptorists

Imprimatur:
Monsignor Maurice F. Byrne
Vice Chancellor, Archdiocese of St. Louis

ISBN 0-89243-309-4
Library of Congress Catalog Card Number: 89–84983

Copyright © 1989, Liguori Publications
Printed in the United States of America
08 07 06 05 04 03   13 12 11 10

Cover and interior art by Chris Sharp

Dedication

Once upon a time there was a little boy who had a basement playhouse where he built magical wonderments and explored the uncharted lands of Someday. He liked frogs and kitty cats. He liked digging dirt and climbing trees. He believed in make-believe and the adventures of the mind. He held my hand and showed me the future. With laughter and love I dedicate this book to that little boy who is now a tall, handsome grownup — my son, Matthew Joseph Snyder.

Introduction

Got a minute? Good! That's all it will take to treat yourself to some fun facts, daffy definitions, and saintly surprises! There's one in here for each day of the year!

Learn about heroes and heretics, papal bulls and bumblebees, ants and can'ts, cannons and cans, lions and legends, and a whole lot more.

Look up today, look up yesterday, look up last week. Look up your birthday, your best friend's birthday, or your unbirthday! But look up! Life is fun. Facts are fun. And so is this book.

Don't wait. Don't hesitate. You'll find an idea to help you meditate and cogitate — on every date! It's great!

January 1

Did you know the calendar the world uses today was put together by a POPE? Did you know the Romans named the first month of the year "January" because of a legend about a two-faced man? Did you know Paul Revere was born on January 1? Did you know it's going to be a lot of fun to find out answers to some questions you never even thought of yet? Read on — and by the end of this year, when someone asks you, "Did you know?" you can answer, "Sure, I know! Do you?"

January 2

In January, when a new year begins, everybody gets a new calendar to keep up with the new days in the new year! But one year everybody got a REALLY new calendar — one that changed around the days and dates! It was called the Gregorian calendar — and you know why? Because it was made by Pope Gregory!
Now even before Jesus was born people had been trying to make calendars, but none of them ever worked quite right. So the Pope decided it was time somebody made a CORRECT calendar! And he did. And it's still in use today! And it's still correct! This year remember Gregory the Pope — and don't mope . . . learn to cope . . . always hope . . . and never say nope! That way EVERY day will be a great day!

January 3

Now what about January and that two-faced man? Well, way back in the time of the Romans, they had a lot of legends and stories. One of them was about Janus, who was supposed to have two faces — one in front and the other in back — so he could look ahead to the future and also could look back at the past. Since a new year is the end of the past year and the beginning of a future year, they thought it would be a good idea to name the first month of the year after Janus — and they named it January. Do you think that was a good idea? Do you look ahead to the future or back to the past? It's a good idea to look both ways — but not at the same time! Remember, you only have ONE face! But what a nice one!

January 4

Today's the feast day of Saint Elizabeth Ann Seton — a lady who never knew when to give up! She was once a beautiful and wealthy young woman who had a good husband and five healthy children. She seemed to have everything; but you know what happened? Her husband got sick and died, his business failed, and she lost all her money. Then two of her daughters died too. She was very sad, but did she give up? She did not! She just worked harder and prayed harder! And you know what happened? She became a teacher and opened the FIRST American Catholic school and then opened the FIRST American orphanage and then founded the FIRST American Order of nuns — the Sisters of Charity. Finally, she also became the FIRST born-in-America saint! Wow! That's a lot of firsts! If you ever feel sad because something bad has happened to you, don't give up. Try again — and maybe YOU can make some "first" things happen too!

January 5

Do you think a saint would ever have a horse named Geraldine? Well, today's saint — John Neumann — did! When he was a young priest, he and Geraldine often rode through the wilderness where the Indians lived! There were no churches there, so sometimes John had to offer Mass on somebody's kitchen table! He also wrote catechisms (books to help children learn about religion) and finally became a bishop and saint! Do you know who YOUR bishop is? Write him a letter today and tell him who YOU are!

January 6

Did you know every month has a special flower? The flower for January is the snowdrop. Its blossoms are as white as snow and it often blooms even before all the snow has melted! If YOU were a delicate flower, would you be brave enough to stick your head up in the cold snow? Sometimes it's hard to do what you're supposed to do, so ask God to help you be brave enough to always "stick up" for what's right!

BRRRR...

January 7

Did you know a tailor could become president of the United States? Today's the birthday of Millard Fillmore, a tailor who sewed and made clothes for people. His family was very poor and lived in a log cabin, but he was ambitious and a hard worker. So he studied law and then taught school and finally became a congressman! In 1848 he was elected vice-president, but only two years later President Zachary Taylor died, and the one-time tailor became president of the United States! Would YOU like to be president? If you were, what would you do to make America better?

January 8

Did you know that each month has a special "jewel"? If you were born in January, your "birthstone" is the garnet. It's a dark red stone and is a symbol of loyalty. Always be loyal — to your family, your friends, and especially to God.

January 9

Did you ever see a "hot air" balloon? Each one is decorated in beautiful colors and designs and is big enough to lift a basket in which several people can ride! It was on January 9, 1793, when the first balloon flight was made in America. A man named Francois Blanchard took off from the yard of the Old Walnut Street prison in Philadelphia and ballooned his way to New Jersey! Would you like to take a balloon ride? You could soar high, high into the sky and look down at the world below. What would you see? Who would you see? When God looks at the world and then looks at you, what kind of person does HE see?

January 10

Brrr! In many parts of the world, January is a month for snow —
time to go sledding, make snowmen, and have snowball fights. Did
you know that no two snowflakes are exactly alike? Every single
snowflake is different and unique — just like every single person is
different and special. No one else is just like YOU! You are different
and special and no one else could ever take your place. So be proud to
be you and always try to be the best "you" that you can be!

January 11

It's another day to fly high! On this day in 1935, a famous
woman airplane pilot named Amelia Earhart took off from Hawaii and
flew to California. This wouldn't be so unusual today, but it was then
because she was the FIRST woman to ever fly solo — all alone —
across the Pacific Ocean. Sometimes it's scary to be all alone, isn't it?
But you know what? You are never REALLY all alone because God is
always with you.

January 12

Did you know that if somebody asks you to "put your John Hancock on this paper," that person wants you to sign your name? That's because John Hancock, who was born on this day in 1737, was the first one to sign his name to America's Declaration of Independence! Others signed it too, but Hancock signed with such big, bold writing that his name stands out more than any of the others! How do YOU sign your name? Practice writing it carefully, because when you sign your name you tell the world who you are. And when you make the sign of the cross, you tell the world you are a Christian! Make the sign of the cross right now and say, "I am a Christian."

January 13

Happy Saint Hilary Day! This saint was a famous preacher and writer who said his job was to defend the teachings of the Church against those "who closed their ears to the truth." Do you ever "close your ears" so you won't hear what you don't want to hear? Open your ears today and listen — and learn!

January 14

Did you know that if people say "You're a Benedict Arnold," that means they think you can't be trusted? Why? Because there was a famous American named Benedict Arnold who became a traitor. He was born on January 14, 1741, and started out to be a loyal American. He was a brave soldier and once led a group of only 500 men against 2,000 enemies and won the battle! But then he got mad because he didn't get as much honor as he expected, and one of his bosses even criticized him. He couldn't take criticism, so to get even he "changed sides" and betrayed America. Everyone was shocked and sad to think such a good leader could do such a bad thing to hurt his country. Do you ever get mad when someone criticizes you? Do you ever do something just to "get even"? You might feel bad when you get criticized, but it would feel even worse to become a "Benedict Arnold."

January 15

Do you know what a "papal bull" is? No, the pope doesn't have a cattle ranch and cowboys in the backyard at the Vatican! But the pope DOES sometimes send out a letter that has some extra special information in it — and to show that this letter is VERY important, he attaches a round lead seal to it. The Latin word for this seal is *bulla*, and that's why these letters have become known as "papal bulls." Rope in some of your friends today by asking them if they know about papal bulls. Won't they be surprised when only YOU know the answer!

January 16

Today the United States takes a holiday to celebrate Martin Luther King's birthday. This famous civil rights leader once made a speech in which he said, "I have a dream. . . ." He dreamed of a world where there would be justice for black people and no more prejudice, a world where ALL people would work together to help each other. Wouldn't that be a great world to live in? Talk to your family or friends today about what the word "prejudice" means and what people could do to get rid of it.

January 17

This may not be a good day to "go fly a kite," but it's the birthday of Benjamin Franklin, who DID fly a kite in a lightning storm because he wanted to learn about electricity. Ben wanted to learn about *everything!* He was the youngest in a family of seventeen children and his parents could only afford to send him to school for a few years, so he taught himself by reading lots of books. Franklin learned so well that he became a printer, postmaster, writer, inventor, scientist, statesman — and one of the most famous men in American history. Do YOU like to read books? A book is like a magic door that can lead you to adventure, knowledge, discovery — and fun too! Wouldn't today be a good day to start to read more books? Leaders are always readers!

January 18

Did you know that nobody can drown in the Dead Sea? Why? Because the water's so salty it's heavy! Instead of sinking you just float to the top. So if you're not a very good swimmer, head for the Dead Sea. Or better yet, take swimming lessons so you can dive in wherever you want. Wasn't it nice of God to invent water so you could have lakes and rivers — and swimming pools!

January 19

Did you ever read a mystery story or watch a mystery movie or TV show? Today's the birthday of Edgar Allan Poe, an author who became famous for writing mystery stories. But do you know what the greatest mystery is? It's God! That's why it's so interesting to be friends with him — and why you can NEVER learn everything there is to know about God!

January 20

On January 20, 1961, John Kennedy became president of the United States and made a special speech. In it he said, "My fellow Americans, ask not what your country can do for you; ask what you can do for your country." What could YOU do for your country? Maybe the best thing you could do would be to live a good Christian life — and pray that all Americans will help their country by reaching out to help each other!

January 21

Today's the feast of Saint Agnes, who is a patron saint of girl scouts. Eat a Girl Scout cookie today and tell God thanks for all the saints who have shown us how to live like "good scouts"!

January 22

Did you know there's a winter bird that canNOT fly but CAN swim? Not only that, this bird looks like it's wearing a tuxedo! Yep, it's the penguin. It has funny little "wings" that it waves around when it runs on land. Those wings are no good for flying, but they're just great for swimming! God sure made a lot of interesting birds, didn't he? They're all sizes, shapes, and colors. If YOU were going to make a brand-new kind of bird, what would it look like? Think about that today and then draw a picture of YOUR bird or write a story about it and give it to your grandma or grandpa or to a special friend or teacher.

January 23

On this day in 1849, Elizabeth Blackwell, the very first American woman to become a medical doctor, received her degree. When she accepted it, she said, "It shall be the effort of my life, by God's blessing, to shed honor on this diploma." She knew that her work as a doctor would be important. But you know what — *all* work is important! So ask God to bless your work too — and to help you to do it well.

January 24

Today is the feast of Saint Francis de Sales, who was a famous teacher, preacher, and writer. One of the things he said was: "You can catch more flies with a spoonful of honey than with a hundred barrels of vinegar." Now do you think Saint Francis was really talking about catching flies — or was he trying to say something else? Do you think maybe he meant that you can make more friends with one little smile than you can with a hundred barrels of frowns? If you've been using too many frowns on your family and friends, surprise them with a big smile today!

BUZZ OFF!

January 25

What would you think of a man who went around capturing Christians and putting them in jail just because they believed in Jesus and he didn't? There was a man named Saul who did that until one day something wonderful happened. God zapped him! All of a sudden one day, Saul realized he had been wrong and the Christians were right! And from that day on he spent the rest of his life going around telling people about Jesus and how to live as a Christian. He even changed his name from Saul to Paul, and today is the anniversary of Saint Paul's change. Is there something in your life you need to change too? Are you maybe too selfish or jealous or grouchy or mean? Do you do what your parents and teachers tell you to do? If there's something in your life that needs changing, don't wait for God to zap you! In honor of Saint Paul, start to change today!

January 26

Today's a double day! It's the feast of Saint Titus **and** Saint Timothy. Saint Timothy was a "best" friend of Saint Paul. When Paul traveled around telling people about Jesus, Timothy would sometimes go ahead — like a messenger — to tell people Paul was coming; and sometimes after Paul left, Timothy would stay behind to continue the work Paul had started. Timothy was a good friend and a good helper. Are you a good friend and a good helper? Can you think of some way you could be a helper today?

January 27

Today's the feast of a lady who knew how to get things started! Her name is Saint Angela Merici, and she is the one who started an Order of teaching nuns who are called the Ursulines. Why don't YOU get something started today? Start a new hobby, start a new friendship, start to read a new book, or maybe even start to clean your room.

January 28

Did you know today is "dumb ox" day? Once there was a boy who was so quiet he hardly ever said anything. He was also very big. And so other children started calling him the "dumb ox"! Boy, were they wrong! Actually, he was so quiet because his brain was busy! After he grew up he became a monk; and when he began to write and to preach, people found out he was one of the smartest "thinkers" in the world. Later he became known as one of the wisest philosophers and teachers in all the history of the Church. His name is Saint Thomas Aquinas and, even though he lived several hundred years ago, the books he wrote are still being used by schools and libraries today! So remember wise Saint Thomas and don't ever be dumb enough to call somebody else dumb!

January 29

Do you know what "serendipity" means? There was an old English fairy tale about three princes who lived in the land of Serendip. As these heroes went adventuring, a curious thing happened. They kept making happy discoveries *by accident* — without planning or scheming or searching! So now it's called a "serendipity" when you "stumble upon" some good luck or a happy surprise! Wish someone a Serendipity Day today! (If no one knows what that means, you can tell the story of the three princes.)

NOPE, NOTHING UNDER HERE BUT SOME DUST BUNNIES AND AN OLD BALONEY SANDWICH.

January 30

Today's the birthday of one of our most famous American presidents — Franklin Delano Roosevelt. One day when he was making a speech, he told the American people, "The only thing we have to fear is fear itself." Do you ever get afraid of the dark and think there might be a monster under your bed? Then when you turn on the light, there's no monster and there was no reason for you to be afraid. Sometimes it's good to be afraid and careful — of mad dogs or traffic or dangerous people or places — but it's not good to be afraid of things that are not fearful! Ask God to help you know when to fear and when NOT to fear!

January 31

You would have liked to meet today's saint — someone who knew how to do magic tricks and walk on a tightrope! Saint John Bosco liked acrobatics and picnics and music — and children! No wonder all the children liked him too. He felt sorry for the poor children in Italy who had no families and nowhere to live; but he had no money to build a house, so he fixed up an old barn and made it into a happy home for homeless children. After that he got other people to help him open more homes and workshops and schools where poor and neglected children could come to live and to learn and to be loved. Saint John Bosco was able to help other people enjoy life because *he* enjoyed life — and he was glad to share his joy. So be like John Bosco today. If you see someone without a smile, give 'em one of yours!

February 1

February is the SHORTEST month of the year — but it's just as important as all the others. A lot of important things have happened in February, and a lot more important things might happen *this* February! If you happen to be short, don't think that makes you any less important than anybody else. People of all sizes and shapes are all part of God's family — short, tall, fat, skinny, loud, quiet, silly, or serious. And that's what makes the world so interesting! So whether you're short or tall, say one prayer today for all the short people in the world — and another prayer of thanks for strawberry SHORTcake and SHORT stories and SHORTwave radio and good baseball SHORTstops!

February 2

It's Candlemas Day! When Jesus was just a baby, Mary and Joseph took him to the Temple because it was a religious custom of that time for newborn babies and new mothers to be presented to God and to receive special blessings. Today that custom is remembered, and in many churches the priest blesses candles — and that's why it's called Candlemas Day! Did you ever hear someone say "It's better to light one candle than to curse the darkness"? That means that instead of always complaining about something you don't like, you should try to "lighten up" and find a way to make it better. Think about that today!

February 3

Did you know it's time to get your throat blessed? According to a very old legend, one day a bishop named Blaise helped a young boy who was choking on a fish bone — and saved the boy's life. Now on Saint Blaise's Day (today) — or on the Sunday of this week —many churches have a blessing of throats. The priest crosses two unlit candles and puts them under your chin and then says a little prayer asking God to bless you and keep your throat healthy. Always remember to be careful when you eat fish so you won't swallow a bone; and be careful when you're tempted to tell a lie because you may have to "eat your words" later!

February 4

The "flower of the month" of February is the delicate, shy primrose — a little wildflower that is one of the earliest flowers to blossom in springtime. Have you ever gone to a park or the woods and looked for wildflowers? You can find some very beautiful "shy" flowers like the primrose "hiding" under a rock or bush in a quiet corner. Some shy people also "hide" in a quiet corner of silence, and the only way you can find out how beautiful and interesting they are is to "seek them out." If you know someone who's shy, talk to him or her and try to make friends. You may be surprised to find that shy friends can be just as interesting as noisy friends!

February 5

And what about this month's "jewel"? Well, if you were born in February, your birthstone is the lovely amethyst. The purple-violet color of the amethyst is often thought of as a royal color! Do you feel royal today? Do you wish you could meet a king and maybe become his friend? Well, you CAN! You can be *best* friends with the greatest king of all! That's right! You can be friends with God, the King of heaven!

February 6

Did you know it was way back in February of 1893 when the FIRST movie studio was built? And you know who built it? Thomas Edison, the man who invented the electric light bulb! It cost him $637.37 to build it at that time, but it would probably cost *millions* to build it today. When movies were first invented, it was so exciting! The whole family could go to the movies together and have a wonderful time. But today some movies are violent and not very nice. When YOU go to the movies, are you careful to go only to the kind of movies Jesus would want you to see?

February 7

Did you ever see the movie called "A Christmas Carol"? It tells about a mean and stingy man named Mr. Scrooge. And that story was written by a very famous writer named Charles Dickens, whose birthday is today! Mr. Dickens wrote many stories about poor children because he hoped that when people read stories about poor children, they would try to help them — and they did! Even people who are mean and stingy like Mr. Scrooge can change and start to care about other people. If YOU care about the poor, maybe there's a little something you could do to help them. Find a small box and make it your "poor box." Whenever you get any extra change, save it in the box; and when the box is full, instead of buying yourself a present, give the money to the poor!

February 8

Do you know what "Ash Wednesday" is? That's a day when you go to church and the priest rubs a bit of "ash" on your forehead to remind you that Lent is beginning. And do you know what is meant by Lent? Lent usually comes in February and lasts for forty days — until time to celebrate Easter. It's a serious time to pray and to think about the time when Jesus died on the Cross to save the world. To thank Jesus, people everywhere try to do something "hard" during Lent. Some "give up" a favorite food — like candy bars or French fries or cookies — and promise not to eat these until Easter. Some even give up watching television! Others pray the rosary daily or do a "good deed" every day. What could YOU do to make this Lent a special time to say "thank you" to Jesus?

> I THINK YOU'RE GOING TO NEED MORE SYRUP.

February 9

Did you ever hear of Pancake Day? That's the day *before* "Ash Wednesday"! Some people call it Mardi Gras — which means "Fat Tuesday"! You know why? Since a lot of people used to "give up" eating ANY kind of rich food during Lent, on the night before Lent began they would use up all the butter and eggs and milk in the house by making *pancakes*! Why don't you ask your folks if you can have a pancake supper this year on the night before Ash Wednesday?

February 10

Did you ever hear of "twin saints"? Today is the feast of Saint Scholastica, who was the twin sister of Saint Benedict. He founded the Benedictine Order of monks and SHE founded the Benedictine Order of Sisters! Remember the twins and be DOUBLY good today!

February 11

Today's the feast of Our Lady of Lourdes. One day in Lourdes, France, a little girl named Bernadette was gathering firewood when suddenly a shining, beautiful lady appeared in the woods and talked to her. It was Jesus' Mother, Mary! She told Bernadette she would like a church built there in Lourdes. At first nobody would believe what Bernadette told them about Mary; but finally they did and they built a lovely church on the spot where Mary had appeared. Ever since, people have come from all over the world to pray together at Lourdes — and many of their prayers have been answered. Say a Hail Mary today to honor Our Lady of Lourdes.

February 12

It's Honest Abe Day! This is the birthday of the great Abraham Lincoln, the man who was president during the Civil War, the man who "preserved the union" so that we would remain the UNITED States of America! Lincoln was famous for many reasons — especially for always being honest. Are YOU always honest? Do you tell the truth, the whole truth? Or do you cheat just a little? A little bit is too much! Be true to yourself and tell the whole truth!

... ONE HUNDRED SiXTY FiVE ZiLLiON, ONE HUNDRED...

February 13

Did you know it takes 120 drops of water to fill a teaspoon? Imagine how many drops of water it takes to make a rainstorm or fill a river! How many drops do you think it would take to make an ice cube or to fill a birdbath or to wash your neck? Have a nice cool glass of water today while you make a list of all the ways you use God's wonderful gift of water!

February 14

Well, of course it's Valentine's Day — time for hearts, poems, and posies. But it's also the feast day of two saints: Saint Cyril and Saint Methodius. Saint Cyril was a monk who invented a Yugoslavian alphabet! Have a bowl of alphabet soup today and see how many words you can spell out — like heart, love, valentine, and saint!

February 15

Suppose you dropped a bag of potatoes and a bag of feathers off a roof at the same time. Which bag do you think would fall the faster of the two? Many years ago a famous scientist named Galileo (whose birthday is today) tried an experiment like this by dropping two things of different weights off the top of the Leaning Tower of Pisa in Italy. To everyone's surprise, both bags dropped at the same speed! Science experiments are often surprising — and important, too. Would YOU like to be a scientist someday? What would you like to discover to make the world better?

February 16

Do you know what the word ''footle'' means? A footle is something silly. And when you footle, you ACT silly or foolish or waste time. Sometimes it's fun to footle, isn't it? But NEVER footle in school — that's against the rule!

No Footle Allowed.

February 17

Did you ever go to a doctor and have him hold a funny-looking thing to your chest and listen to your heartbeat? Well, that funny-looking thing is called a stethoscope, and it was invented by a French doctor named Theophile Laënnec, whose birthday is today. But do you know where he got the idea for this invention? Well, one day Dr. Laënnec was watching some children playing with a board. One child would tap very softly on one end of the board while another listened at the other end. The sound of the tap came out much louder after it had traveled along the board. This gave the doctor a bright idea — a new and better way to hear the soft sounds of heartbeats! Say a little prayer for your doctor today, and the next time you see him, ask him if he knows who invented the stethoscope.

February 18

Do you know what an ''adder'' is? No, it's not someone who says ''two plus two equals four''! An adder is a poisonous snake that is mentioned several times in the Bible. Beware of adders — but be glad you have good teachers who teach you how to add! If you didn't know how to add, you couldn't add up how many cookies you ate today, how many nickels you get in your allowance, or how many good things you have in your life! Say a prayer for one of your teachers today.

February 19

Do you think the sun moves around the earth — or the earth moves around the sun? Many years ago, people thought the earth was the center of the universe, but a man named Copernicus (whose birthday is today) discovered that the earth — like other planets — revolves around the sun. People made fun of Copernicus and refused to believe him for a long time, but he was right. He had made one of the most important discoveries in history! Tonight when it gets dark, look out your window at all the stars. Only God knows how many there are. Only God knows about all the planets in the universe. Only God knows all about YOU! That's because God *made* the stars and the universe and you!

February 20

On February 20, 1962, John Glenn became the first American astronaut to orbit the earth. His space capsule was named Friendship 7. Today think about something nice you could say about one of your *friends* — and then say it!

February 21

Tomorrow is George Washington's birthday — but it might be celebrated today or maybe it was celebrated yesterday or the day before! Why? Because now America celebrates Presidents' Day on the third Monday in February. Years ago Washington's birthday was celebrated on February 11, but the new Gregorian calendar (which you read about on January 2) changed it to February 22. So you can have a "real George" time celebrating all during February! Bake a cherry pie, make a cherry cake, plant a cherry tree — and put on a cheery face!

25

February 22

This is the feast day called "The Chair of Saint Peter." The chair? Well, back in the early days of the Church, each Christian would celebrate a "spiritual birthday" — the day he or she was baptized into the Church. In the same way, a bishop celebrated the day he became bishop and took over the bishop's chair in his cathedral. Today we celebrate the occasion of Saint Peter taking over the "chair" as head of the Church on earth. Do you know what day YOU were baptized? Ask your folks to tell you all about the day you were baptized — and then celebrate your "spiritual birthday" every year!

February 23

Sing a song today to celebrate the birthday of a famous musician named Handel, the man who wrote some of the beautiful music you hear in church at Christmas and Easter. His most famous work, "The Messiah," is played by symphony orchestras all over the world. Do you ever listen to symphony music? It's always fun to try something new, so turn on the radio today and listen to a "classical music" station. It's not rock, but don't knock it until you hear it! You might LIKE it!

February 24

It was in February 1879 when a man named F. W. Woolworth opened his first five-and-ten-cent store. Most of the things in the store only cost 5¢ or 10¢! After a few years, there were Woolworth stores in almost every big city in America. Today it would be hard to find something that only costs five or ten cents in ANY store; but did you know that even five or ten cents is still valuable to the very poor people in mission lands? The Church sends money to help them and also sends missionaries — priests, Sisters, Brothers, and laypeople — who teach the people about God and try to make their lives happier. Would YOU like to be a missionary someday?

February 25

When the weather's freezin', you hear a lot of sneezin'! And when you sneeze, sometimes somebody says Gesundheit — the German word for health. Do you know why? Many years ago there was a terrible illness that spread all around the world, and many people died. Those who caught this ''plague'' started to sneeze — so a sneeze was a serious thing! People would wish them good health, praying that God would help them get well. Whenever you hear about somebody who's sick, always say a silent little prayer for their health!

February 26

Today's the birthday of ''Buffalo Bill'' Cody — who galloped across the western plains, rounding up buffalo, scouting for the Comanche Indians, and delivering mail for the Pony Express in the dangerous days of the Wild West. It isn't as dangerous to deliver mail now, so why don't you do something wild today and write a letter to the president of the United States? Tell him what you like or don't like about the way he's running YOUR country!

27

February 27

Do you know any poems? "Roses are red . . . violets are blue . . . frogs are good friends . . . and so are you!" That's a silly poem! But there are a lot of beautiful poems; and some of them were written by Henry Wadsworth Longfellow, a famous American poet who was born on this date. Why don't YOU write a poem today — about your best friend or your family or maybe even about God? You could have a good *time* putting together a *rhyme*!

February 28

Since yesterday was LONGfellow's birthday, make a list today of all the LONG things you can think of. Did you know the LONGEST river is the Nile? And the LONGEST bridge is the Golden Gate Bridge in San Francisco? And the day that SEEMS the LONGEST is usually the day before any school vacation! Wonder why?

February 29

Here's a little calendar poem for you:

Thirty days hath September . . . April, June and November . . . All the rest have thirty-one . . . Except for February alone! For February, twenty-eight is fine . . . till leap year gives it twenty-nine!

Every four years February gets an EXTRA day. So whenever leap year comes around, rejoice in your extra day — and do something extra special with it!

March 1

March into March by doing what schoolchildren do in Britain on the first day of the month! When you start to speak to someone — before you say anything else, you must say "white rabbits"! Imagine how surprised people will be when you say, "White rabbits — good morning, Mom," "White rabbits — pass the milk," or "White rabbits — wait for me!" March is the month when you might see wild rabbits chasing around your lawn to celebrate the glory of God's glorious spring! (And you might have someone chasing YOU around the lawn if you say "White rabbits" once too often!)

March 2

"Oh, say can you see . . . '' TOMORROW is National Anthem Day! On March 3, 1931, ''The Star-Spangled Banner'' officially became America's national anthem. Do you know all the words of this song? If you start TODAY to learn them, then tomorrow you can sing a star-spangled song all day long to show everyone how happy you are that God chose you to be born an American!

March 3

Ring, ring, it's ding-a-ling day! Today's the birthday of Alexander Graham Bell, the man who invented the telephone. What would your life be like WITHOUT a telephone? Maybe it would be better — if you are a ding-a-ling on the phone! Today, think of ways you could ''reach out and touch someone'' if you DIDN'T have a phone. What could you do *right now* to ''reach out'' to someone?

March 4

March's ''dancing'' flower is the jonquil. It has pretty yellow or white blossoms and sometimes looks like it's dancing in the garden as it waves about in the springtime breeze. Do YOU feel like dancing or prancing today? Springtime is such a happy time when all the buds on the trees and flowers are coming out to remind everyone of new life — just like Easter reminds the world of the ''new life'' of Jesus after he rose from the dead!

March 5

If you were born in the month of March, your ''jewel'' is called a heliotrope. Isn't that a pretty name? The stone is dark green with little spots of bright red. Maybe because of the red spots, some people call it a *bloodstone* — and maybe that's also why your birthstone symbolizes courage. Have courage today — and every day. Whenever someone tries to get you to do something that you KNOW is wrong, have the courage to just say NO!

March 6

Look UP today — to celebrate the birthday of Michelangelo, a famous artist who painted some of the most beautiful pictures in the world on the CEILING of a chapel in Rome, Italy! God gave Michelangelo a great talent — just as he gave each and every person a special talent. What is YOUR talent? What do you do well? What do you *like* to do — write, draw, sing, play soccer, study, dance, smile? Whatever your talent is, resolve today to always USE it. If you don't use it, you could lose it!

March 7

Did you know the first book ever printed was the Bible? It was called the Gutenberg Bible because it was Johann Gutenberg who invented a new kind of printing and then opened the *first* print shop — so he could print the Bible! Do YOU ever read the Bible? Ask someone in your family to help you read something from the Bible today and talk about what it means. ·

March 8

Did you know that when glass breaks, the cracks move faster than 3,000 miles per hour? That's much faster than a jet airplane can travel! That's even faster than YOU can run! Did you know some children run *very* fast when they're going out to play but move *very* slowly when their mom or dad calls them to help with a chore? How fast do YOU run when you're called to help?

March 9

Happy feast day, Saint Frances of Rome — the saint chosen to be the "patroness" or protector of people who drive cars! Did you know you can get your family car *blessed?* Ask your folks to invite a priest to dinner and then ask him to bless your car! OR ask your family to hold hands in a prayer circle before dinner tonight and say a little prayer to ask God to protect your family on the highways and byways!

March 10

Woooooooeeee . . . do you feel a little spooky today? Maybe that's because it was in March 1818 when the first book about FRANKENSTEIN was published! One night a lady named Mary Shelley was with some friends, and they decided to have a contest to see who could tell the best spooky story. Mary couldn't think of a good story that night, but LATER she got the idea for a *really* spooky one. She wrote it down and got it published, and people today are still getting scared by her Frankenstein monster. Do YOU like to make up stories? Make up one today — but instead of a spooky one, make up a *funny* one! Then tell it to someone and LAUGH together! A laugh is the best way to chase away spooky worries!

March 11

It's Johnny Appleseed Day! Once there was a man named John Chapman who liked nature and animals. He did a lot of traveling, and everywhere he went, he planted some apple seeds. Soon lots of apple trees grew up and had lots of nice, juicy apples on them for people to enjoy — and Mr. Chapman became known as Johnny Appleseed! Did YOU ever plant any seeds and watch them grow? It's fun, isn't it? But did you know you can plant the *seeds* of God's love by being kind and thoughtful to other people? Plant some seeds today and ask your folks if maybe you could have Johnny Apple(no)seed pie for supper!

Hot dog anyone?

March 12

On March 12, 1912, a lady named Juliette Low invited some young girls to come to her house for a tea party. That afternoon she showed them pictures of a girl's club in England called "The Girl Guides." They began talking about how much fun a club like that would be, and by the end of the afternoon they had started the very first chapter of the Girl Scouts of America. Why don't you invite some "good scouts" to your house today for a tea party? If you don't like iced tea, serve punch and cookies or hot dogs or cold cucumbers! Then think about what YOU could do to become a "good scout" for God!

March 13

Sit back and enjoy a cool drink today to celebrate the birthday of Joseph Priestly, the man who invented "sparkling" water! That led to the invention of soda pop, colas, uncolas, and all those nice, sparkly drinks you like! Today's a good day to think about what you could do to put more SPARKLE and fun into your family life. Maybe you could ask your folks to have a "Family Night" each week — or each month. On Family Night you could always do something *together;* you could play games or go out for pizza or swap jokes or share what your "secret dreams" are or sing songs — and maybe even end the evening with a little prayer asking God to bless you and keep your family together!

March 14

Once upon a time, a man named Eli Whitney worked very hard to make enough money to go to school to learn to be a teacher. And then he traveled to a distant city where he had been promised a job. But Mr. Whitney was out of luck! When he arrived his teaching job had been given to someone else, and the only other work he could get was in the cotton fields! Picking and cleaning cotton was slow, hard work, and Eli thought there must be a BETTER way for it to be done. So he started planning and finally invented the "cotton gin" — a machine that could clean cotton faster than 100 people working all day long! He received a patent on his invention on this day in 1794, and after that the United States became the greatest cotton producer in the world! Eli's bad luck had turned into good luck! The next time something "bad" happens to you, don't get discouraged. Remember that sometimes something that seems sad later turns into something glad!

March 15

Today's the feast of a very special saint who started planning to become a priest when he was just a little boy — but had to wait thirty-four years to achieve his dream. When Saint Clement Hofbauer was finally ordained a Redemptorist, he was chosen to cross the Alps to bring his Congregation's work to Poland and Austria. He was a missionary, a preacher, a teacher — and also a baker! One day when he was begging food for some homeless boys, he came to a bakery where there was only one baker trying to do all the work alone. The priest rolled up his sleeves and helped bake bread all day long! Then the grateful baker gave him plenty of bread for the hungry boys. When YOU see someone who needs help, don't loaf! Give 'em a slice of your time or some of your "bread." That's what Saint Clement would have done!

March 16

Are you good at math? Then think about this saying: "Friendship doubles your joy and divides your grief." What do you think that means? Well, if you have a friend to share happy times, then you have TWICE as much fun. And if you have a friend to share bad times, then you'll only feel HALF as sad. Be friendly to someone today! To HAVE a friend, you have to BE a friend!

March 17

Do you have anything green to wear — a shirt, sweater, suspenders, or socks? Then wear that green today to help the Irish celebrate Saint Patrick's Day! One day someone asked Saint Patrick to explain the mystery of the "Blessed Trinity." Saint Patrick reached down and picked one of the green shamrocks that grow in Ireland. The shamrock has three leaves on ONE stem, and Saint Patrick explained that was like the Father, Son, and Holy Spirit — three persons but only ONE God! Say a special prayer to the Trinity today — and if you don't know one, you'll find one on May 25.

March 18

Did you know there's a bird named a *plover* and a flower named a *clover*? The plover and the clover can be told apart with ease . . . by paying close attention to the habits of the bees. . . . Everybody knows the bee can be in clover, but as you can plainly see, there is no "b" in plover! Today, tell God thanks for making so many interesting birds and flowers for you to discover!

I MUST BE A BIRD. THERE'S NO B IN ME. I ONLY EAT WORMS.

WORMS!? YICK...

March 19

Do you know anybody named Joe or Joseph? Well, today's Saint Joseph Day! Joseph was a carpenter who hammered nails, sawed wood, made tables and chairs, and fixed things that got broken. But Saint Joseph had even more important work to do — God had given him the job of taking care of Jesus and his Mother, Mary! Saint Joseph lived in a little town, worked hard, and never got rich or famous, but he never complained. He was happy because he knew he was doing the work God wanted him to do — and THAT was the most important job in the world! Do you complain too much? Don't grumble and mumble. Be humble — like Saint Joseph. And you'll be happy too!

March 20

It's time for a tongue twister! Can you say this **very** fast? "Billy Button bought a buttered biscuit. If Billy Button bought a buttered biscuit, where's the buttered biscuit Billy Button bought?" Does your tongue ever get twisted enough to make you say something mean or hateful to somebody else? The next time that happens, untwist your tongue and say "I'm sorry" — and then keep your lip zipped!

March 21

Spring has sprung! It's the time of year for the "vernal equinox" — a fancy way to say a time when the day is as long as the night! Spring into action today! Ask your folks if you can do some yard work — rake up old leaves, pull up new weeds, plant some seeds. Then "plant" yourself on your knees on the ground and ask God to help you always *protect* his beautiful earth.

March 22

Did you know a lemon is a berry? Well, according to botanists (the people who study plants), it is! This big yellow berry is "berry" sour when you bite into it, but it can be "berry" good when you use it to make lemonade or lemon pie! Do you know anybody who ACTS like a lemon — all sour and grouchy? Try to think of some sweet surprise you could give that person — a piece of bubble gum, a picture you drew, a bunch of flowers, a jelly doughnut. Maybe a few sweet surprises could turn that lemon person into a lemonade person!

MAYBE THIS WILL SWEETEN YOU UP. YOU OL' SOURPUSS.

March 23

Did you ever hear of Angel Falls? Now, how could you hear an angel fall when an angel has wings? Well, Angel Falls is the name of the highest waterFALL in the world. It's in Venezuela and was discovered by a man named Angel. Did you ever hear of a "guardian angel"? It is said that when you are born, God gives you a special angel all your own — to guard you and help you. It's sort of like having your own personal lifeguard or bodyguard. Isn't that a nice idea? If you could SEE an angel, what do you think YOUR guardian angel would look like?

March 24

While you're thinking about angels, wouldn't this be a great day to learn a "guardian angel" prayer? How about this one: "Angel of God, my guardian dear . . . sent by God to protect me here . . . all through this day be at my side . . . to keep me safe, to guard and guide."

March 25

Think about angels one more day! The Bible has a LOT to say about angels. One of the stories it tells is about a young girl named Mary who was saying her prayers one day when suddenly an angel came into the room and talked to her! The angel said, "Hail, Mary" (that means Hello, Mary). And then the angel *announced* or told her that God wanted her to be the Mother of Jesus! That's why today's feast is called the "Annunciation," or announcement day. Mary said she would do whatever God wanted her to do, and so she became Jesus' Mother. Do you know the "Hail Mary" prayer? Announce to your family that you should all say a Hail Mary together in honor of this happy day!

March 26

Do you feel "scrappy" today? Then make a scrapbook! Staple together several pieces of construction paper to make a "book" and print this title on the cover: What It Means to Be a Christian. Then get out some old magazines and cut out pictures of people who are acting the way YOU think Christians should act. Paste these pictures onto the construction paper — and you've made a book! Show it to your folks or teacher and explain why you think each picture shows *what it means to be a Christian.*

March 27

Do you think Superman is the only one who has X-ray vision? Nope! Today's the birthday of Wilhelm Konrad Roentgen, the man who discovered how to use X-rays to help sick people. Using his invention, doctors can take pictures of the INSIDE of a person to see WHERE a person is sick — and this has saved many lives! Pretend today that YOU have X-ray vision: Pick out someone and try to see how that person must feel INSIDE! Do you think he or she feels sad, happy, mad, hurt, lonely? What would that person wish or hope for? It's good to get to know someone the same way God does — from the inside out instead of from the outside in!

March 28

Did you know that names have special meanings? For example, Peter means *rock,* Marcia means *from Mars,* David means *beloved one,* and Nancy means *graceful one.* If you could change your name to the name of a saint, what name would you choose? Could you be as *saintly* as that saint?

March 29

Did you know that in Calama, a town in the country of Chile, it has NEVER rained? Wouldn't it be a Calama-ty if it never rained in YOUR town? There would be no water to drink, no way to wash the dishes or go swimming or clean your muddy feet! You'd have to carry in or pipe in water from some other town — what a job! Say a prayer today to thank God for the wonderful gift of rain!

March 30

On this day in 1858, Hyman L. Lipman patented the first pencil with an ERASER! Isn't it wonderful to have an eraser so you can rub out your mistakes and start over? Wouldn't it be great to have an eraser that could rub out mistakes you make in life? Well, you DO have one! It's called the Sacrament of Penance; by confessing your faults you become reconciled to God and others. When you make a mistake, tell God how sorry you are and promise to try never ever to make that mistake again — and God will forgive you! Isn't that the BEST kind of eraser?

March 31

Did you know that when you write down a date, everything that happened BEFORE Jesus was born is lettered B.C. (Before Christ) and everything that happened AFTER Jesus was born is lettered A.D. (the Latin abbreviation for *Anno Domini,* which means "*in the year of our Lord*")? Julius Caesar was born in 100 B.C. George Washington was born in A.D. 1732. When were YOU born?

HE MAY LOOK NEANDERTHAL, BUT I'M SURE HE WAS BORN A.D.

April 1

It's April Fools' Day — a day when people play silly tricks on each other and then say, "April Fool!" They're not mean or hateful tricks — just funny, silly ones. What kind of a trick could you plan today? While you're thinking, think of this: Some people thought Jesus was a "fool"! You know why? Because he CHOSE to be poor when he could have been rich . . . he "turned the other cheek" when he could have fought and won . . . he even suffered and died to save the world. Tell Jesus thanks today for being a loving "fool."

April 2

Today's the birthday of Hans Christian Andersen, a wonderful storyteller who wrote lots of stories for children. Turn off the TV tonight and read a fairy tale or a fun book! OR there's another book where you can find lots of exciting stories — the Bible! Why don't you ask your folks to read a Bible story with you tonight?

April 3

Did you know the name for this month — April — possibly comes from the Latin word *aperire* which means "to open"? This is the month when umbrellas open up for April showers and buds open up for spring flowers! It's a good time for YOU to "open up" — to new ideas! Get out the dictionary — and go through the pages, looking for words you've never heard before! Can you find "infinitesimal" or "conjecture" or "rebuttal" or "colossal"? You may want to make an infinitesimal conjecture or a colossal rebuttal today!

April 4

Go to the head of the class today — to celebrate the feast of Saint Isidore of Seville, who is sometimes known as "The Schoolmaster of the Middle Ages" because he wrote an encyclopedia! Yesterday you looked through the dictionary; today look through an encyclopedia! You'll be surprised at how many interesting and strange things you can find in there! Then say a prayer to thank God for the fun of new words and new ideas.

April 5

Did you ever hear of Booker T. Washington, the famous black leader and educator? In April of 1856 he was born to a Virginia slave family. He studied and worked hard; and when only twenty-five years old, he was chosen to head a school called the Tuskegee Institute. Under his leadership it grew from two old buildings to a modern school with over one hundred buildings — a place where many black students got a fine education and a good start in life. His birthday is a good time to ask yourself how you feel about people who have a different color skin, speak a different language, or come from a different neighborhood. Did you know they are ALL members of ONE family — God's family, YOUR family?

WE MAY BE ALL ONE FAMILY, BUT I HOPE I DON'T HAVE TO DO THE DISHES FOR 'EM ALL!

April 6

How do you think it would feel to stand "on top of the world"? That's where the explorer Robert E. Peary stood on this day in 1909. He was the first man ever to travel across the snow and ice to reach the North Pole, the TOP of the world! Do YOU like to explore? Explore IN YOUR MIND today! Imagine what it might be like to live on a desert island or in an African jungle. And remember that no matter where you are — a desert, a jungle, or the North Pole — God is there to explore with you!

April 7

Today's the feast of Saint John Baptist de la Salle, a priest who had a lot of "new ideas" about teaching two hundred years ago! Instead of teaching one child at a time, he thought it would be a good idea to put several students together in a classroom! His method became popular in France, in Italy, and then all over the world! Say a prayer today for good teachers everywhere!

April 8

Two men who signed the Declaration of Independence were born on this day — William Williams in 1731 and Lewis Morris in 1726. The document they signed changed the world — and dramatically changed the lives of people in the United States! It's great to be independent — but did you know it's also important to be dependent? Sometimes you NEED someone you can depend on, lean on, and ask for help; and other people need to depend on YOU, too! Everybody needs somebody sometime!

April 9

Did anyone ever tell you that "you look fresh as a daisy"? Well, that fresh-looking flower is the flower for April! Daisies have a yellow center with white petals, and you might see them in a garden or just growing wild by the side of a road! Some girls have the same name as this pretty spring flower. Do you know anyone named *Daisy?* Do you know anyone with the same name as any OTHER flower? Think of some flower names, pick out the one you like best, and then thank God for your favorite flower!

April 10

Many states celebrate today as Arbor Day. And do you know what *arbor* means? That's the "botanical" name for TREE. So today's the day to plant a tree! OR — if you don't happen to have a tree ready to plant — you could LOOK at trees today! Go around your neighborhood and see how many different trees you can find! Maybe you could collect one leaf from each tree and bring them home and look at them. How are they alike? How are they NOT alike? Isn't it wonderful how God made so many different kinds of trees — and flowers — and people?

April 11

Saint Stanislaus, who died on April 11, 1079, was a bishop of Cracow, Poland. About 900 years later, ANOTHER bishop of Cracow became world-famous when he was named Pope John Paul II. Say a prayer today for the pope and Church leaders all over the world — asking God to help them guide their people in the right direction.

April 12

Can you guess what the "jewel" for April is? Some ladies wear it on their left hand, next to a wedding ring. And it has the same name as the field where you play baseball! Yep, it's the diamond! If you were born in April, your "birthstone" is one of the most *precious* in the world! And YOU are precious to God! Remember that today.

April 13

Today's the birthday of Thomas Jefferson, a man famous for MANY accomplishments. One of them is known as the Louisiana Purchase. When Jefferson was president, the northwest part of our country was still owned by France. THEN Jefferson "made a deal" and bought from France all the land from the Mississippi River to the Rocky Mountains and from the Canadian border to the Gulf of Mexico! Overnight the size of the United States doubled! Get out a map today and see if you can figure out the part of the country that's so big you could spend YEARS traveling across it, "discovering" rivers and mountains, cities and towns, deserts and lakes — and churches and schools!

April 14

Here's a riddle for today: What kind of room has no walls, no door, and no floor? A MUSHroom! Do you like to eat mushrooms? If you've never eaten any, ask if you can have mushrooms for supper some night! Even if you don't LIKE them, it's still fun to sample the tastes of all the vegetables God gave the world. Yum, yum.

HE'S DEFINITELY NOT A FLOWER.

April 15

Did you know God made a bird named a crow and a flower named a crocus? And how can you tell a crow from a crocus? The crow makes lots more NOISE! Do YOU make lots of noise? Noise can be lots of fun; but quiet can be fun too! Try to be VERY quiet today! Whisper. Tiptoe. Close doors softly. And find a quiet spot to sit for five minutes and LISTEN — listen to the sound of God's birds or breeze or . . . ?? What do you hear?

April 16

Is today the birthday of Wilbur Wright? That's right! He and his brother Orville were the famous Wright brothers who built the first airplane that could really fly! Take a flight of fancy today! Lie on the ground or sit in a lawn chair and look up at the clouds. See what pictures you can imagine in the clouds — a giant taking a nap, a gorilla eating a banana, a smiling face, a frowning face? Relax and giggle at all the funny things you can imagine when you have your "head in the clouds"!

April 17

It's time for the Name Game again (see March 28)! Did you know that the name Albert means "noble and brilliant," Nora means "light, bright one," Gregory means "watchful," and Bernadette means "brave as a bear"? Why don't you pick out one of those names and ACT that way today! Which will you be today: brilliant, bright, watchful, or brave?

April 18

In Indochina there is a plant with such large leaves that children use them for UMBRELLAS in the April showers. Did you know God's love is like an umbrella — protecting and shielding you? Never leave home without it!

I CAN'T SEEM TO GET MINE OPEN.

April 19

Did you know it is impossible to sneeze and keep your eyes open at the same time? Even if you DON'T sneeze today, close your eyes and try to walk across the room. See how hard it would be if you were in the dark all the time? Thank God today for the special gifts of sight and light.

April 20

Did you ever see a cuckoo clock? Did you notice that when the clock hands get to a new hour, a little door opens and an artificial bird pops out of the clock to chirp "cuckoo!"? Today is celebrated as Cuckoo Day in some places in Europe because this is the time when REAL cuckoo birds can be seen in the trees. But the cuckoo is a LAZY bird! Instead of building a nest, the cuckoo lays its eggs in some OTHER bird's nest! Don't be a lazy cuckoo! Pick up, straighten up, and clean up YOUR "nest" today.

April 21

It's the feast of Saint Anselm, a very wise scholar and teacher, who is sometimes known as the "father of scholasticism." Would YOU like to be a teacher someday? Make a list today of all the things you think you need to be a *good* teacher. Then maybe you would like to show the list to your teacher and talk about it!

April 22

Did you ever notice a nickel, peer at a penny, eye a dime? Try it! You'll find written on each coin the words "In God We Trust." Those words have been imprinted on American coins ever since that motto was approved by Congress on April 22, 1864. Do YOU trust in God? You may think that God does not answer your prayers, but he always does. Sometimes the answer is yes; sometimes the answer is no. And sometimes you have to wait a long time before you get an answer. But you WILL get one. Trust in God.

April 23

Did you ever watch an old, old movie on TV starring a little girl named Shirley Temple? Back in 1937, only six people in the whole United States earned more money than she did — and she was only nine years old! To celebrate her birthday today, think about what YOU would do if you earned lots of money. Would you spend it all on yourself or would you share it? How would you spend it? How would you share it?

April 24

It's the feast of Saint Fidelis Sigmaringen, who was nicknamed "the poor man's lawyer." Would YOU like to be a lawyer someday? Why? If you COULD be a lawyer or a judge, what would you do to help the poor?

April 25

This is the feast day of Saint Mark, a man who might be called a SECRETARY to Saint Peter. Since Peter had been a good friend of Jesus, he was always telling wonderful stories about the things that had happened when Jesus was on earth traveling around with his apostles. And since Mark was a good friend of Peter, people started asking Mark to write down the things Peter said so they could remember them. Mark did this, and now you can read those stories about Jesus in the Bible today. Ask your folks to get out the Bible today and read some of the things Mark wrote.

April 26

Today's the birthday of a bird watcher! When he was a little boy, John James Audubon liked to explore in the woods, where he discovered that birds came in all sorts of sizes, shapes, and colors. He learned how to sit very, very still so the birds would come close enough for him to get a really good look at them. And then he decided to draw sketches of birds — to show how each one differed from the other. People were SO surprised by his sketches because they had never looked at birds that closely before. When he grew up, Audubon became the most famous ''bird painter'' in the world! Would YOU like to be a bird watcher? Could you sit that still? Put out some birdseed or breadcrumbs in your backyard today and watch God's birds have a picnic!

April 27

Did you know roller skates were first invented in April of 1760? A young man rolled into a party in London wearing wheels on his shoes and playing the violin! Since he hadn't learned how to skate very well yet, he didn't know how to stop and smashed into a mirror! He made a smashing entrance, didn't he? The next time you put on skates, imagine what it would have been like if God had made all people with wheels on their heels! It might have been fun for a while, but it would have gotten irritating to keep rolling into others and falling down! Tell God thanks for giving you feet instead of wheels!

April 28

Today in 1919, a brave man leaped out of an airplane. He was testing the very FIRST parachute! And it worked. The parachute opened and he floated down through the sky and landed safely back on earth. Do you ever get scared the first time you try something new? It CAN be scary; but that's the only way to keep learning and to keep growing.

April 29

Saint Catherine of Siena, whose feast is today, came from a poor Italian family, but when she grew up, she did important work for the pope! She bravely wrote letters to the kings and queens of Europe asking them to help the pope, and she traveled around Italy talking to people who were AGAINST God and convinced them to be FOR God. Do YOU ever talk to others about God and tell them how wonderful he is?

April 30

On April 30, 1904, the famous St. Louis World's Fair opened, and the fairgrounds lit up like a dream world with hundreds of electric lights. That wouldn't be unusual today, but it was in 1904 because that was the FIRST time most people had EVER seen an electric light! It was also the first time the fairgoers had ever tasted hot dogs, iced tea, and ice cream cones! Can you imagine what the world must have been like BEFORE electric lights and ice cream? Aren't you lucky you were born AFTER they were invented!

May 1

"**M**ayday! Mayday!" Did you know you can use this call as a signal that you need HELP? That's what radio operators do when a ship at sea or a plane in the air has an emergency; they use their radio to send a MAYDAY message! But when YOU feel troubled or have a family emergency, you can also send for a different kind of help by saying a quick little prayer — like "Dear God, I love you and I need you. Please help me today."

May 2

"**M**ay Day" has another meaning too! The first day of May signals the beginning of the month when special honor is paid to Mary, Jesus' Mother and the Mother of the entire Church. A lot of families honor Mary by having a May altar in their home. Ask your folks to help you find a good spot — like a small table in the corner or a shelf in your room. Put a statue of Mary there and add a pot of flowers, a candle, or anything to make it look pretty. Ask everyone in the family to stop there every day and say a Hail Mary.

May 3

May is also the month when you honor your own mother! The second Sunday of every May is Mother's Day, a time to say thanks to moms by giving them a card or a little gift like candy or a bouquet of flowers. But did you ever hear of a "spiritual bouquet"? It doesn't cost any money and you can make one like this:

SPIRITUAL BOUQUET
5 prayers
5 good deeds
5 smiles instead of frowns

Make a card and decorate it with drawings or stickers and maybe even a poem. Explain to your mom that the "spiritual bouquet" means that you will say five prayers asking God to bless her; do five good deeds to help her (set the table, take out the garbage, or do some other chore); give her five smiles of cooperation instead of frowns and complaints. If you want, you can think of other "spiritual" things to add to the list; but then don't forget to DO whatever you promise! Your mom just might be so surprised she'll think this is the best "bouquet" ever!

May 4

Could you eat soup with a fork? No, of course not! But did you know that for hundreds of years people couldn't eat ANYTHING with a fork because there weren't any? Even kings and the richest people ate all their food with spoons, knives, and fingers! Thank goodness forks finally became popular about two hundred years ago so now you can eat salad with a fork and save fingers for sandwiches! But before each meal, remember how blessed you are to have good food to eat and take a minute to thank God. You can simply say, "Thank you, God, for this food" or you can make up your own special "blessing" prayer.

May 5

Pax vobiscum! Do you know that those words from the old Latin Mass mean "Peace be with you"? Today most Masses in the United States are said in English so you can understand the words; but you have to LISTEN to understand and then pray along with the priest. Of course, God understands ALL languages, so when you pray — whatever you say, in whatever language you use — God will listen AND understand.

May 6

On this day in 1840 the first postage stamp was issued in England. You probably don't think much about postage stamps, but imagine what it would be like if you didn't have stamps or post offices. You couldn't get birthday cards or Christmas cards or letters or packages! Today would be a good day to write a letter to your grandma or grandpa or make a homemade card and send it to someone who is sick or lonely. Wouldn't they be surprised! You could even tell them that you're writing them today because this is the birthday of the postage stamp!

May 7

A famous musician, Johannes Brahms, was born on this day in 1833 — and you've probably heard a song he wrote! Although he became famous for writing symphonies, he also wrote a song called a lullaby. When you were just a baby, someone probably sang Brahms' Lullaby to you to lull you to sleep! But you're not a baby now, so it's time to learn about some other beautiful music. Next Sunday really listen to one of the songs sung at Mass and start trying to memorize the words so you'll know how to sing along. Maybe you've been to a party where they played musical chairs — well, at church it's musical prayers! That's what church songs (or hymns) are, you know — musical prayers!

May 8

The thirty-third president of the United States, Harry S. Truman, was born on this day in 1884. He once said, "Some of the (American) presidents were great and some weren't. I can say that I wasn't one of the great presidents — but I had a good time trying to be one." Remember that not everyone can be great — but you can have a good time TRYING to be great!

May 9

What does Cleopatra have to do with the month of May? Well, one of Cleopatra's favorite jewels was the green emerald, and that's the "jewel" for this month. If you were born in May, you may want to wear an emerald "birthstone" ring someday. The "flower" for the month of May is the hawthorn. Isn't it wonderful how God made so many different jewels and flowers? Look around your backyard today and see how many "treasures" you can find that were made by God! You might find a pretty rock or an unusual leaf. You might look to the sky and watch the birds or clouds. Thank God for the unending variety of beauties he used to decorate your world.

May 10

Did you ever play "funny face"? Look in a mirror and what do you see? Someone who looks just like you! Make a funny face and that face in the mirror will make one too! Make a sad face and the face in the mirror will get sad too. Play peekaboo, stick out your tongue, frown, wink; whatever you do, that other face will be doing it too! But now take a really good look at that face. You may or may not like what you see, but God made that face and he loves you JUST THE WAY YOU ARE. Be glad and say thanks to God for giving you eyes to see, ears to hear, teeth to chew, lips to smile, and eyebrows to raise in happy surprise.

May 11

St. Augustine said, "The world is a book, and those who do not travel, read only one page." Would you like to travel and "read" the rest of the world? How would you journey — by car, plane, bus, or train? For many years, trains were the most popular way to travel across America and across many parts of the world. Did you ever hear the WHOOEEE sound of a train whistle in the night or watch a train clickety-clacking along a railroad track? Think about trains today — and think about how a family is like a railroad train! Each car of a train is hitched to the next car, and all the cars have to pull together if they're ever going to get anywhere. That's the way it works with a family too — if you want to get places and have a happy trip, you've gotta pull together!

May 12

Did you ever hear of "The Lady with the Lamp"? That's the nickname that was given to a famous woman, Florence Nightingale, who was born on this day in 1883. She was from a wealthy family and could have led a life of luxury — but she wanted to lead a life of service! So she studied nursing and became the head of a large hospital in England. When war broke out, Florence took some of her nurses right to the battlefield to help treat the wounded. No woman had ever done that before! Since there was no electricity back then, the LADY would take her LAMP and sometimes work all through the night to be sure the wounded received proper care. And because of her work and dedication, many soldiers who would have died were saved. So remember this Nightingale. Remember that valuable luxuries can make your life fun, but helping others can make your life valuable!

May 13

Did you ever hear of a little town called Fatima, in a country called Portugal? On this day in 1917, in a field near that little town, three children were taking care of a flock of sheep when an extraordinary thing happened. Mary, our Blessed Mother, came to talk to them! She asked them to tell people to say the rosary frequently and to pray for sinners and for the conversion of Russia. Now there is a beautiful shrine and church built near the place where Mary came to talk to the children, and people come from all over the world to pray there. Since today is the feast day of Our Lady of Fatima, think about Mary. What would you say to her if she came to talk to YOU?

May 14

Did you ever have a fever and get your temperature taken with a thermometer? Well, you couldn't tell how hot your fever was if it wasn't for an inventor who was born on this day in 1686. His name was Gabriel Daniel Fahrenheit. He wasn't satisfied with the thermometers of his day because they just didn't work right! So he experimented and put mercury inside a thermometer instead of the alcohol that was used before. That simple change made all the difference. HIS thermometer was accurate every time! Fahrenheit's discovery was a big help to doctors and to weathermen and to everybody! When you have a temperature, your head gets hot; and when you have a bad temper, you are called a hothead! Don't be a hothead! Keep your "cool" today and every day.

May 15

Today's the feast of Saint Isidore the Farmer. This Spanish saint worked as a farm hand; but as he walked behind the plow, he prayed. He loved animals and said that everything he saw on the earth reminded him of God and his goodness. In Mexico, this day is celebrated by farmers who decorate their animals with flowers to honor the saintly plowman. Ask your folks if you can have your own celebration today. Invite friends to come over and bring their pets for a yard party. Decorate each pet's collar with flowers and have some pet "treats" and some people "treats"! Sit in a circle and talk about all the funny things your pets do and then join hands to say a prayer of thanksgiving for kitty cats and kangaroos, puppy dogs and panthers, lions and llamas, turtles and tigers, and all the wonderful animals with which God gifted the world.

May 16

Did you ever hear of Seward's Folly? William Henry Seward was born on this day in 1801 and became Secretary of State when Abraham Lincoln was president. Seward negotiated for our country to buy a huge piece of land to the north for a little over seven million dollars. Many people criticized him and called the land Seward's "frog pond." But Seward became famous for that purchase because his "folly" turned out to be one of the biggest bargains in history and became our fiftieth state — the vast, wealthy state of Alaska! Sometimes you might be tempted to criticize or make fun of others because you think they are doing something foolish — but later you may find out they were right and you were wrong. Ask your mom to celebrate Seward's birthday today by treating you and some friends to Eskimo Pies! While you're munching, you could talk about Eskimos and Alaska and seals and snow and Mr. Seward.

May 17

Did you ever hear of a May "crowning"? Maybe you've even been to one at church — but you can have one at home too! Many years ago, heroes would often be crowned with a garland of flowers or green leaves as a sign of honor. Today the Church honors Mary in this same way during this special month of May. If you have a May altar (as suggested on May 2), measure the head of the statue of Mary and then make a tiny crown of real or artificial flowers to fit the head. Ask the family to gather and have a procession through the house. Start at the front door and end at the altar, singing a "Mary" song as you process. At the altar, "crown" the statue of Mary and then all kneel together to say a decade of the rosary or three Hail Marys.

May 18

Did you know there are seven sacraments in the Catholic Church? You probably DID know that, but if somebody asked you to name them and you wanted to be a champ and name them right off, could you do it? Well, here's a little secret — just remember the words BE CHAMP! B for Baptism. E for Eucharist. C for Confirmation. H for Holy Orders. A for Anointing of the Sick. M for Matrimony. P for Penance. That isn't the order in which they are usually listed, but it's sure an easy way to remember them when you want to *be a champ*!

May 19

Did you ever use a computer? A computer can be fun and interesting and can do amazing things! But do you know what the greatest computer on earth is? It's the human brain! You can ''program'' your brain to make your body talk, walk, laugh, cry, and even pout! Think about all the wonderful things you can think about! Then tell God you think he's wonderful to make such a fabulous computer — just for you!

May 20

It's Fly High Day! On this day in 1927, Charles Lindbergh took off in a one-seater airplane; and when he landed the next day in Paris, France, thousands of people were there to celebrate his happy landing. Why? Because he was the very first person to ever fly across the Atlantic Ocean — all alone all the way from New York to Paris! Celebrate today by drawing pictures of airplanes, making paper airplanes, watching the sky to see how many airplanes fly over your house in an hour, and dreaming about where in the world you would like to fly if you had your own airplane. Even if you never fly anywhere in your whole life, you can give thanks that God gave you the gift of imagination — so you can dream and use your imagination to take ''flights of fancy'' anytime, anywhere!

May 21

Today is the feast of one of the newer saints — Saint Crispin, who was the first saint canonized by Pope John Paul II on this day in 1982. As a young boy Crispin learned to be a shoemaker, but then he decided to become a Capuchin Brother. At the monastery he was assigned to do a lot of little jobs; he was a cook, worked in the garden, begged for donations, and did whatever ordinary things needed to be done. But everyone loved him for his wisdom and goodness. Sometimes you hear about saints who did big, heroic things and you might think you could never do anything like that. But you COULD do what Saint Crispin did — help your family and friends and do whatever little ordinary jobs need to be done without complaining or wishing somebody ELSE would do them. That's a good way to begin to be a saint!

May 22

Some things are square, some are round. Some things start and stop, some things go on forever. How many things can you think of that are round like a circle — a tire, a doughnut, a lifesaver, a ring? Now think about God's love. It's like a circle — no beginning, no end. God's love for you will never stop. It goes on forever.

May 23

Did you know the first bubble gum was called Blibber-Blubber Bubble Gum? It wasn't successful because the bubbles kept bursting — so its inventor, Frank Fleer, went back to work. He chewed and blew and gummed and bubbled for about twenty years; but finally, in 1928, by gum, he did it! He invented the very successful Double Bubble Gum! Sometimes it might seem like things are going wrong for you, too, and your bubbles keep bursting: You try for a home run and strike out, you study hard and still make a bad grade, you try to be good at home and get blamed for something you didn't do. Well, you just have to keep on working and trying and praying, and maybe someday your double bubble dreams will come true too!

May 24

Did you know that the words ''What hath God wrought!'' were the first words sent by Samuel F. B. Morse on his new invention — the telegraph? This happened on this day in 1844, and it began a new Communication Age. For the first time people could send messages across long distances. Soon there would be many other inventions to help people talk to each other and communicate faster. But no one could improve on the way you can communicate with God. You can talk to him anytime, anywhere — and you don't need a telegraph or a telephone! All you need is your brain and your heart!

May 25

Today's the feast of a saint with an unusual name — Bede, the Venerable. He was a monk who became a famous writer and historian and was the first one to use the words *Anno Domini* or A.D. to date events. He was given the title "Venerable" to honor his wisdom and learning, but his favorite prayer was a simple one. Maybe you know it. If you don't, maybe you'd like to memorize it: "Glory to the Father, and to the Son, and to the Holy Spirit, as it was in the beginning, is now, and will be forever. Amen."

May 26

Ha, ha, ha! Today we honor Philip Neri, a saint who was known for his laughter and his happy look at life. Make someone smile today by telling a joke or a riddle. If you don't have one, try this riddle: When young cows go out to eat, where do they go? Answer: To a calf-a-teria!

May 27

Did you ever think about what a wonderful gift God gave you when he invented the voice? Think about all the things you can do with your voice: sing, shout, whisper, talk, hum, yodel, laugh. Use your voice today to praise God. Sing a happy song, whisper a prayer, talk to someone about God and his goodness and his greatness.

May 28

Did you know it took eleven years just to grind and polish the mirror in California's Palomar telescope, now the second-largest telescope in the world? With this instrument, scientists can photograph objects in the sky that are sextillion miles away from earth and then track the objects throughout the night as the earth turns. What a wonderful invention! But it's not nearly as wonderful as the stars and planets and universe which God invented! Go out tonight after dark and just look up at the sky and the stars and think about all the wonders out there, still unexplored, still unknown — except to God.

May 29

Patrick Henry was born on this day in 1736 and became a lawyer, a governor, and a member of the Continental Congress at the time of the American Revolution; but he is remembered most for one thing he said. Do you know what that was? He said, ''Give me liberty or give me death.'' America DID win its liberty, and today's Americans are very lucky to live in a land where they are free to vote, to live or work or go to school where they choose, and to worship God without being persecuted. Say a prayer today for all the people who live in countries where freedom is only a dream.

May 30

Did you ever hear of Saint Joan of Arc, whose feast day is today? She was a shepherdess who lived a quiet, simple life with her family. But her homeland of France was at war, and Joan began to pray very hard for her country and for the soldiers who were fighting to save it. One day she heard God telling HER to go and save her country. At first she couldn't believe God wanted her to do this, but she kept hearing this message, so finally she put on armor and rode a horse and led the frightened French soldiers into battle — and on to victory! This is a good day to pray for brave people everywhere and to ask God to help you be brave too!

May 31

Did you know there's a Historical Museum of Spaghetti in Italy? Yes, there is! And there's a Money Museum in St. Louis, Missouri. All over the world there are many kinds of museums where you can go to see how things used to be, are now, or might be in the future. But there is one thing that will never change, from past to present to future. Yesterday, today, or tomorrow — God's love was, is, and always will be with you.

June 1

Today's a day to be fair and JUST — to celebrate the feast of Saint Justin, whose name means just that. Of course, you should try to be just and play fair EVERY day, shouldn't you?

June 2

Be *creative* today as you celebrate the birthday of Leonardo da Vinci, one of the greatest creative geniuses of all time. His paintings are known as masterpieces, but he was also an inventor, engineer, sculptor, and architect! Over five hundred years ago, when most people had never dreamed of such things, he designed a submarine, a parachute, and a flying machine! God gave this man a brain filled with NEW ideas — and da Vinci USED his brain. Do YOU use your brain as much as you could or should?

June 3

Mmmmm . . . did you ever smell the sweet odor of a honeysuckle blossom? June's flower of the month has a honey-sweet smell that perfumes the summer air as it vines along fences or walls or winds up a tree! Bees come to get nectar from the yellow, white, or red blossoms, and birds eat the berries that grow on the vine after the blossoms fall off — so this is a ''working'' flower that provides food for others. How could *you* be a honey of a worker too? You could help cook supper tonight!

THE WHOLE TRUTH AND NOTHING BUT THE...

June 4

Did you know it was in June of 1843 that a Black woman named Isabella quit her job and changed her name to SOJOURNER TRUTH? A sojourner is a person who stays somewhere for only a short time and then journeys on — and that's what Isabella did as she traveled about the country telling people about the problems and needs of Black people. Her new name — and her work — became famous. Think of the bravery of Sojourner Truth and promise yourself that you'll tell the truth — today and every day!

June 5

It's the feast of another traveler — the missionary, Saint Boniface, who is known as the "Apostle of Germany" because he traveled around Germany teaching people about Christianity. The word **bonny** means handsome or beautiful — so remember Saint Boni-face today and put on a HAPPY FACE!

June 6

It's fun to have fun, but sometimes you are supposed to do MORE than that! Today's the feast of Saint Norbert, a rich nobleman who thought about becoming a priest but put it off because he was enjoying his luxurious life too much. Then one day he was struck by lightning — and this got his attention! After that he worked very hard for the Church and became a bishop and a saint! Is there some work you think you SHOULD do — but you keep putting it off? Wouldn't this be a good day to DO it?

June 7

In June of 1683 the FIRST museum was opened in England — and people were charged according to how long they stayed in the building. If they liked it enough to stay and look longer, it cost them more than if they only liked to look a little! Have YOU ever been to a museum? Ask your folks today if you can start planning a ''family field trip'' to a museum.

June 8

June is the month for Father's Day, so it's time NOW to think ahead! Who will receive a present from you on Father's Day — your dad, your grandpa, an uncle, a friend, or maybe the ''Father'' who's the pastor at your church? Any ''father'' would enjoy getting a homemade Father's Day card. And maybe you would also like to make a scrapbook for your dad. You could paste in cartoons about fathers (clipped from a newspaper or magazine), family snapshots, pictures you've drawn — and then write in a few paragraphs about ''What My Dad Means to Me.'' Start today and you'll have your cards or presents ready in time to make it a Happy Father's Day!

June 9

If you were born in the month of June, you have a very interesting "birthstone." June's "jewel" is the agate, a stone harder than steel! It's striped with many colors — white or gray, brown, yellow, blue, or black. Sometimes YOU have to be harder than steel too! When somebody else is trying to get you to do something that you *know* is *wrong*, you have to act like an agate; and no matter how hard it is, do what you KNOW is RIGHT!

June 10

Summertime is the perfect time for a picnic in the park! Have you ever gone on a picnic where people played tug of war? You get two teams who face each other and hold on to a rope. Then each team tries to pull the rope away from the other team. That can be fun on a picnic, but it's not so much fun in a family — when brothers or sisters or mothers or fathers are always pulling AGAINST each other. The way to be a *happy* family is to love each other enough to PULL TOGETHER! Ask your folks to go on a family picnic soon — and tell them about the tug of war!

June 11

Do you know who had the LARGEST family in the world? George Washington — because he was the ''Father of his country''! Say a prayer today for the president, the members of Congress, and for all leaders — and ask God to help YOU be a good leader too!

June 12

Take a flower to lunch today! Go out in the yard and pick a flower — any kind of flower, even a dandelion! While you're having lunch, get acquainted with the flower. Really look at each part — the color, the shape of the petals, the kind of leaf it has. If God went to so much trouble to make even a tiny flower so carefully, think how careful he must have been when he made something as special as YOU!

June 13

Today's the feast of Anthony of Padua, a saint who is sometimes known as ''the finder of things that are lost''! When people lose something, they sometimes say a prayer to ask Anthony to help them find what they are looking for. Did you ever LOOK for something? When you LOOK at people, do you see all the good things about them or are you too busy seeing the BAD things? Start today to always LOOK for the GOOD in others!

June 14

Hip, hip, hooray — for the red, white, and blue! Today is Flag Day! The flag is an important symbol of our country, so everyone should always have respect for it. Every time you see an American flag passing by in a parade, put your hand over your heart and whisper a little prayer: "God bless America."

June 15

In June of 1888 George Eastman introduced the Kodak #1 — his FIRST box camera. To use this camera, the owner had to take one hundred pictures and then mail the camera back to the factory! At the factory they would develop the pictures, reload the camera with film, and then mail it back to the owner. Wouldn't this be a great time to have a family photo party? Get a camera and plenty of film and then take turns making crazy poses! You might even want to dress up in funny clothes or hats. It will be a lot of fun taking the pictures — and even more fun when they are developed and you can look at them together and put them in your family album!

June 16

Did you ever realize that the Bible is a family album? When you look at *your* family pictures, your folks can tell you what it was like "way back when" you were a baby — and maybe even when your parents and grandparents were babies! Well, "way back when" Jesus was born, there were no cameras, but the Bible has stories that are like "word pictures" that tell you what it was like when the family of the Church began. Aren't you glad you belong to TWO families — your own and God's?

June 17

It's HOORAY FOR YOU Day! Make a list of all the good things about YOU. Whisper to God and tell him all the things you like about the way he made you and ask him to help you BE all the things he MADE you to be.

June 18

On this day in 1903, two people decided to drive from California to New York in one of the newfangled ''motor cars.'' It took them sixty-one days to make the trip! Today you can drive from coast to coast in only a few days — or fly from California to New York in just a few HOURS! If you could travel anywhere in the world, where would you like to go today? Travel there in your imagination, and when you get there, tell God thanks for putting so many different kinds of places and people on the planet Earth.

June 19

This day in 1910 was the very *first* time Father's Day was celebrated. It's nice to be nice to fathers on Father's Day, but wouldn't it be nicer to try to be nice to them on other days too?

June 20

After the Declaration of Independence, Congress appointed three men — Benjamin Franklin, Thomas Jefferson, and John Adams — to design an official "seal" for the newly formed United States. On this day in 1782, their design for the Great Seal was approved. And do you know what motto they put on the seal? It's *E Pluribus Unum* — Latin words that mean *out of many, one*. This reminds you that the United States is many states and many people joined together to make one country. To get a good look at the Great Seal, look for the great eagle on a one-dollar bill. You'll see *E Pluribus Unum* written on a ribbon in the eagle's mouth!

June 21

Happy birthday to America's FIRST First Lady — Martha Washington! Say a prayer today for the First Lady of the United States — and for the "first lady" in every American home!

June 22

Did you ever hear the song about Casey Jones and his railroad adventures? Ask someone to tell you the story about Casey today, and then think about how a family is like a railroad train! Each car is hitched to the next car, and all the cars have to pull together if they're ever going to get anywhere!

June 23

Today in 1834 a U.S. patent was obtained for a "submarine diving suit"! The suit was made of airtight rubber. A brass helmet rested on the shoulders and had an airhose to connect to a ship. And the shoes were weighted with lead so the diver could sink down far enough to see all the wonderful surprises under the water! Today's scuba gear lets divers easily swim under water and delight in the wonders which God put there thousands of years ago, just waiting to be discovered someday. If you can't go deep-sea diving today, maybe you could go exploring at the library — to discover a "fish book" with pictures of the many interesting things that can be found in God's underwater world.

June 24

Do you ever listen to an announcer on radio or TV? Well, today's the feast of a very special ***announcer*** — Saint John the Baptizer. Before Jesus began his work on earth, God gave John the very special job of announcing or telling everyone that Jesus was coming! John went from town to town, and many people listened to him. When they showed they were ready to welcome Jesus, John baptized many of them. That's why he is called John the Baptizer. Suppose YOU were an announcer with the job of telling people about Jesus for the very first time! What would you say to describe Jesus and Christianity?

June 25

Did you ever hear those exciting adventure stories of the days when there were knights who wore suits of armor and who lived in castles? Each knight had his own coat of arms — a design that was used on his shield or flag to identify him. The design included emblems that would stand for who and what he was — for example, a lion for bravery, a flower that symbolized his family, the color blue to show loyalty. If you were making a design, what emblems would tell about you — a baseball bat, a hamburger, a schoolbook, a skateboard, a friend? Why don't you make yourself a coat of arms today and hang it up for all to see!

June 26

If you had fun making your coat of arms yesterday, why don't you ask your family to help you make a FAMILY coat of arms today? You could all discuss and vote on what is most important to you as a family. Would it be your home, your car, your Church, your pets, a golf club, a flower, a certain color? Draw your family coat of arms and hang it up next to the one you made yesterday!

June 27

Since you got your family "up in arms" yesterday, ask them today to help you design a coat of arms for your Church! Decide what is most special to you as the family of God. Would it be a cross, the Bible, wedding rings, a rosary, a chalice, a host, a certain prayer book? Draw your Church's coat of arms and hang it up too. Now pretend you're a knight in shining armor and look at your three coats of arms. Did you really choose the right things to represent your family? Are the things you chose the things that should REALLY be important — or should there be something more important to you? Think about that this week.

June 28

June is the month when there are lots of flowers and lots of weddings! Did you know ladies wear their wedding rings on the third finger of the left hand because people once believed there was a nerve that went from that finger right to the heart? Have you ever gone to a wedding? Did you know Jesus went to a wedding once? Ask someone to help you find the place in the Bible where it tells the story about Jesus going to a wedding at a place called Cana — and then read all about the miracle Jesus performed there.

June 29

Today is the feast of a fisherman! In fact, this is a DOUBLE feast — a day honoring both Saint Peter, the fisherman and Church leader, and Saint Paul, the preacher. This would be a good day to go fishing OR to have a tuna fish sandwich for lunch! It would also be a good day to say a prayer for all of today's Church leaders who "fish" for people — to bring them into God's Church.

June 30

June has busted out all over! On this LAST day of the month, make a list of thirty reasons to thank God for the thirty days of beautiful June! The summer moon . . . sunshine at noon . . . ice cream in a spoon . . . breezes to blow a balloon . . . a fun tune. . . .

July 1

On this day way back in 1847, United States postage stamps went on sale for the very first time! There were only two kinds of stamps — one cost five cents and had a picture of Benjamin Franklin on it, and the other cost ten cents and had a picture of George Washington. Today, why don't you write a letter WITHOUT a stamp — a letter to God! What would you like to tell him — about you or your family or your school or your world?

July 2

Do you know what job Superman had when he wasn't leaping tall buildings in a single bound? He was a reporter — and this summertime would be a good time for you to become a reporter too! Start today to be a July ''spy''! Pretend you have been sent on assignment to get a true-life story for a newspaper or TV station! Wherever you go, take a pencil and paper — or a tape recorder if you have one. Interview your grandma or grandpa, older relatives, or neighbors or friends. Ask questions like: ''What was life like when you were young? Was school different in those days than it is today? Who was your best friend? What was your favorite toy? Ask about the Church too — what they remember about weddings, baptisms, processions, or holidays — and whether anything was different than it is today. Write down or record all the stories, and then at your next family get-together, present your own ''family news broadcast''!

July 3

There's no doubt about it — today is the feast of doubting Thomas! When the other apostles told Thomas that Jesus had risen from the dead, Thomas said he'd have to see it to believe it! Later he DID see Jesus and DID believe, but because of that one ''doubtful'' remark, this poor apostle got stuck with the nickname *doubting Thomas*! Did you ever doubt and wonder about things? Well, there's one thing you NEVER have to doubt about — you are a child of God and God loves you!

July 4

On this day in 1884 the people of France presented a wonderful gift to the people of America. Do you know what it was? The Statue of Liberty! Wouldn't it be nice if somebody gave you a very special gift — something you could enjoy and treasure enough to make you careful to keep it safe? Well, somebody DID give you a gift like that — God made the world and gave it to you! Think of all the ''treasures'' of the world today and thank God for them.

July 5

Today's saint — Anthony Zaccaria — thought people shouldn't leave all the church work to be done by priests and Sisters and Brothers. He said *everyone* should get busy and help! What could YOU do to ''help out''? Maybe you could get your friends together and start a ''Call-on-Me Club''! Tell the pastor to ''call on you'' whenever he needs some work done — cleaning up the yard, running errands, whatever. A helper club could be fun!

WE'RE ON OUR WAY.

July 6

July's a lazy, hazy month when it's fun to just float in a pool or a lake and take it easy — and that's just what this month's flower does! July's flower is the water lily — a large, beautiful flower that grows in water instead of in the ground! Frogs like to use a water lily for a "chair"; they jump up on one and sit there, croaking and blinking and watching the world float by. Pretend you're a water lily today, floating quietly and happily on a lovely lake — not mad or sad, not busy or hurrying, just cool and serene, enjoying the soft summer day. (But watch out for funny frogs!)

July 7

Do you know what the July "jewel" is? If you were born in July, your "birthstone" is one of the most expensive of all the precious jewels. It's the sparkling deep-red RUBY. Make today a red-letter day! Have a bowl of red strawberries. Make a salad with ripe red tomatoes. Make a list of all the things you can think of that God made and then colored red!

July 8

Today's the birthday of John D. Rockefeller, a poor boy who grew up to become one of the wealthiest Americans of his time. When he retired from business, he had a fortune of over a BILLION dollars. But before he died he gave away most of his wealth to charity. If you had a billion dollars, how much of it would you give away? No matter how rich or poor you are, it's good to remember to share with others.

July 9

Sew what's new today? This is the birthday of the man who invented the sewing machine. Elias Howe watched his wife sewing things by hand and decided he would make a machine that could make sewing easier and faster. People laughed at his idea, but after five years of work in his machine shop, he got a patent on his invention and it changed forever the way the world makes clothes. Would you like to be an inventor? Think today of what you could invent to change the world!

July 10

Did you know God made a bird named a parrot — and a vegetable named a carrot? Both are made in bright and happy colors and both can result in squawks! A parrot TALKS in squawks, and some children SQUAWK every time they see carrots on a dinner plate! But carrots are good for you and parrots are fun for you; so don't squawk — give thanks for both!

July 11

It's the feast of Saint Benedict, an abbot who was known for his knowledge of Scripture and Church music. The word "benediction" means a blessing — so when you say a blessing before each meal this week, ask your folks if you can also read a short Scripture quote or sing a short Church song in honor of Saint Benedict!

July 12

Did you know this is the birthday of Julius Caesar — who was born on 12 Quintilis, 102 B.C.? Back when Caesar was born — 102 years *before* Christ — this month was called Quintilis! But after Caesar grew up and became a famous Roman conqueror, the month of his birthday was renamed to honor him, and it became known as JULY. Seize Caesar's day today and become a CONQUEROR! Make a list of your bad habits or things you would like to change about the way you act. Then plan how you can CONQUER just ONE of them!

July 13

Hooray for Saint Henry, whose feast is today. He was a duke who later became an emperor! He was wealthy, but he gave much of his wealth to the Church. He was important and powerful, but he was never too busy to find time to pray every day. Do YOU pray EVERY day?

July 14

It's time for a watch-the-weather party! Tomorrow is Saint Swithin's Day, and according to an old English legend, if it rains tomorrow it will rain for the next forty days! But if it does NOT rain tomorrow, it will NOT rain for the next forty days! Invite some friends over tomorrow to watch the weather. If it does NOT rain, turn on the sprinklers and go running through the pretend rain! If it DOES rain, get out some umbrellas and go ''singin' and dancin' in the rain''!

July 15

Say ''Happy Birthday'' to Mother Cabrini — the FIRST U.S. citizen to be named a saint! Think of all the people who live in the world today. Do you think any of them will be named a saint someday? Do you KNOW anyone you think might be a saint?

July 16

Oops . . . yesterday was the birthday of a famous artist named Rembrandt. Many of his paintings showed people and happenings from the Bible; but — surprise — he painted the faces of the people from the Bible to look like the faces of his own friends! Wasn't that a funny idea? When you hear stories from the Bible, do you ever try to picture in your mind what the people looked like? How do you think Saint Peter looked? Or Jesus' Mother, Mary? Or Jesus?

YOU PAINT A PRETTY GOOD PICTURE.

July 17

Here's a tongue twister for you today. Say this VERY fast: "Willie Winkle wiggled and wigwagged in his wagon. If Willie Winkle wiggled and wigwagged in his wagon, where is the wagon where Willie Winkle wiggled and wigwagged?" Never ever wigwag or wiggle in church because, if you do, that might worry somebody else who would start to wiggle too — and if everybody was busy wiggling, nobody would have time to pray!

July 18

A man named William Makepeace Thackeray was born on this day in 1811. He was from a wealthy family and liked his life of luxury, but suddenly his fortune was lost! For the first time in his life he had to EARN a living! He tried several different jobs and failed in all of them. Finally, in desperation, he tried to become a writer; and he became so famous that his books are still studied in schools today! If Thackeray hadn't had the "bad" luck to lose all his money, he would never have become a great writer! So whenever something "bad" happens to you, ask God to help you turn it into something good!

July 19

Did you know that in Washington, DC, there are more telephones than people? Since Washington is the nation's capital, there are lots of government offices with lots of telephones there — plus lots of people who have extra phones in their homes! It's OK to be a telePHONE who likes to talk on the phone, but resolve today to NEVER be a phony or fake!

July 20

Do you know how to do the "moonwalk"? The FIRST moonwalk was made on this day in 1969 at 9:56 P.M. (E.D.T.) when American astronaut Neil Armstrong stepped out of his spaceship and onto the surface of the moon. Do you know what he said? "That's one small step for man, one giant leap for mankind." Think today about how the earth is just one tiny speck in one galaxy of the great universe made by God. Isn't it wonderful to know that the God who made the moon and stars made you too — and knows you and loves you?

July 21

It's the feast of Saint Lawrence of Brindisi — a saint who could speak and read EIGHT different languages! Think of all the people of the earth and all the different languages they speak — German, Italian, French. . . . How many can you think of? Would you like to study one of those languages someday and travel to a faraway land where people speak a language that is NOT English?

July 22

The Bible has been called *the greatest story ever told.* What is the GREATEST thing that ever happened to you? Ask your friends and family to tell you about the GREATEST thing that ever happened to them. And give thanks to God for all the GREAT things in life!

July 23

It's the birthday of James Gibbons, the Cardinal who helped start — and then laid the cornerstone of — the Catholic University of America in Washington, DC. Would you like to go to college someday? What kind of college do you think you would like the most? What would you like to study? What would you like to be when you grow up?

July 24

Summertime's family vacation time — and map time! Whenever you go somewhere you've never been before, you have to get a map to find out what roads to travel and what turns to take! Whether or not you're going on a vacation this year, why don't you make a family map today? Instead of mapping where you're going, map where you've already been! If your family has moved a lot, draw in the different cities or neighborhoods where you've lived. If you haven't moved, draw in important LANDMARKS — the apple tree in the backyard, the ice cream store on the corner, the church where you were baptized, the house where your grandparents live. . . . This can be your TREASURE MAP — a map of treasured memories!

July 25

Bang the drum, shout and stomp — to celebrate today's feast of Saint James, the Apostle. Jesus nicknamed him and his brother, John, "sons of thunder." Sometimes it's fun to "thunder about" — making noise and having fun, but sometimes it is NOT. Do you know which time is which?

July 26

This is a good day for grandparents! It's the feast of Saint Joachim and Saint Ann — and since they were the parents of Jesus' Mother, Mary, you might think of them as Jesus' grandparents! Do you think Saint Ann made cookies for Jesus and Saint Joachim took Jesus fishing? Say a prayer for YOUR grandparents today — and maybe you could also make a homemade "surprise hello" card for them or give them a surprise hello phone call!

July 27

In July the hummingbirds fly! Did you ever watch them? You have to look fast because they can swoop away in a second! When they stop to get some nectar from a flower, they don't perch — they hover! And their tiny wings move so fast they make a little humming sound. Make today a humming day — hum as you work, hum as you play, hum as you lie in the hammock, hum as you have a ham sandwich! Tell God thanks for hummingbirds and have a humdinger of a happy day!

July 28

Did you ever hear of the Great Wall of China? Three hundred years before Jesus was born, the Chinese decided to build a wall around their whole country! Since that meant they had to make a tall wall 14,000 miles long, it took them a thousand years to finish building it! Do you ever "build a wall" around yourself — and get mad and pout and not let anybody "in" to talk to you or to try to make it better? Resolve today to NEVER build a wall too tall for somebody to reach over it to give you help and a hug!

July 29

Today's the feast of a saint who was a good friend of Jesus! Her name was Martha, and she lived with her sister, Mary, and their brother, Lazarus. Jesus would often come and stay at their home and visit with them and have dinner with them. Since Martha was the one who usually cooked the meal, she has become known as the "patron saint" of cooks, housewives, and hotelkeepers. Do YOU like to cook? What would you serve if Jesus was coming to YOUR house for dinner tonight? He WILL be there, you know — because he is ALWAYS with you.

July 30

Did you ever take a ride in a Ford automobile? Today's the birthday of Henry Ford, one of the first men to build a "horseless carriage" — one that was run by a motor instead of being pulled by a horse! On his first job, Ford made $2.50 a week, but he soon became one of the most famous men in the automobile industry! How's YOUR motor running today? Rev it up, get in gear, and pretend you are driving down the road to the future. Where are you going? What are you going to do when you get there?

July 31

It's the feast of Saint Ignatius of Loyola — a man whose life was changed by a cannonball! He was "driving down the road of life," planning to have a career as a soldier, UNTIL one day he was wounded by a cannonball! While he was getting well he had nothing to do, so he read the story of the life of Christ. This interested him so much that he next read stories of the lives of the saints. When he got well, he went to a special shrine and hung up his soldier's sword and gave his life to Christ. He started a new Order of priests called the Jesuits and lived such a good life that he became a saint! Don't wait for a cannonball. Start today to try to be more SAINTLY!

August 1

Can you imagine getting a college degree and becoming a lawyer when you are only sixteen years old? That's what Saint Alphonsus Liguori did! But after a few years as a lawyer, Alphonsus (whose feast is today) decided to *switch careers* and become a priest, a writer, and the founder of the Congregation of the Most Holy Redeemer, the Redemptorists. What would YOU like to do BEFORE you're sixteen years old? Make a list today of all the things you'd like to do BEFORE and AFTER your sixteenth birthday!

August 2

On this day in 1889 the city of San Francisco, California, was invaded! Not by enemy soldiers, but by millions of crickets! Did you ever hear ONE cricket chirping in your backyard? Can you imagine how much noise MILLIONS of crickets would make? Probably more noise than YOU could make! What OTHER sounds have you heard in your backyard — a kitty cat's meow, a dog's bark, a bird's song? Aren't you glad God gave you a voice instead of only a chirp or a bark?

August 3

On this day in 1492 Christopher Columbus set sail from Spain with a fleet of three small ships — the Niña, the Pinta, and the Santa Maria — on a journey to discover a new route to India. When he sighted land, at first he thought he had found India instead of the New World of America. That's why he called the natives ''Indians''! And that's what they've been called ever since! This would be a good day to read a book about Indians (they have many different tribes and interesting customs) and say a prayer for Indians everywhere!

August 4

Do you remember that the month of July was once called Quintilis but was renamed July to honor Julius Caesar? Well, August was known as Sextilis but was renamed to honor Caesar Augustus. What would YOU have named this summer month that is filled with warm days, sunshine, lots of flowers and fresh vegetables? Sumtime? Suntime? Warmuary? Flowerember? Vegust?

August 5

Some families use a charge card to buy-now-pay-later. Other families use cash to pay-as-you-go. But does your family ever pray-as-you-go? Whenever your family takes a little vacation or goes on a long drive, suggest to them that you start the trip with a little prayer, asking God to help you have a safe journey. Some families say a rosary-on-the-road together. Others say an Our Father or some other favorite prayer. Wherever you go, whenever you go, remember to pray-as-you-go.

August 6

On August 6, 1926, Gertrude Ederle became the first woman ever to swim the English Channel — all the way from England to France. She was in the water fourteen hours and thirty-one minutes! During that time, people in a tugboat followed along, and whenever Gertrude got tired, she would float on her back and sip hot chicken broth which was ''served'' to her from the tugboat! Do you think you could swim for over fourteen hours without stopping OR sip chicken soup while floating on your back? Take a swim today and thank God for giving you MUSCLES so you can bend an arm, breathe, kick a leg, swim, and sip soup!

August 7

Did you ever eat a poppy-seed roll — a dinner roll that has delicious tiny black seeds on top of it? If you did, you ATE part of the flower for August — the poppy! This beautiful large flower has brilliant red or yellow blossoms and its seeds are used in cooking, so it's as useful as it is pretty. The next time you go to the grocery, ask your folks if you can buy some poppy-seed rolls and TASTE the flower of August!

August 8

It's the feast of Saint Dominic, whose ideal was to "speak only OF God or WITH God." No foolish talk for him! Are you careful how YOU use God's name? Sometimes today you hear people in movies or on TV use God's name in a way that is NOT holy — and isn't that a shame? Why don't you start a Family "Holy Name" Society and ask all your family — and friends too — to promise that EVERY time they use God's name they will say it with love and reverence.

August 9

The "jewel" for August has a mysterious-sounding name; it's called the sardonyx. If you were born in August, your "birthstone" is a double stone! It's an onyx with stripes or layers of dark red sard, which is a form of quartz. Did you know some people have "layers" too? Some persons seem dumb in math but are smart in history; some act silly but have serious thoughts; some look nice on the outside but may not be very nice on the inside. What kind of layers do you have?

August 10

Saint Lawrence, whose feast is today, worked for the pope in the early days of Christianity. He was told to sell some of the Church's possessions and give the money to the poor. When the Roman ruler heard about this, he was furious and demanded that Lawrence bring all the rest of the Church treasures to him. Saint Lawrence agreed but said he would need three days to collect the treasures. Three days later Lawrence surprised the Roman ruler by bringing him many of the poor, the blind, the orphans, and the needy people of the city. He told the Roman ruler that THESE were the REAL treasures of the Church! Did you ever think of poor, unfortunate people as "treasures"?

August 11

Did you know there's a "patron saint" of television? Her name is Saint Clare and her feast is today! Television is an amazing scientific invention and it's fun to watch, isn't it? But some of the programs are not so nice — so be careful what you watch today and every day.

August 12

Did you ever hear the story called "Goldilocks and the Three Bears"? Today's the birthday of the man who wrote that story — Robert Southey. He was a famous poet and writer, but people remember him most for his story of the bears and their chairs and the porridge that was too hot, too cold, or just right. Do you ever grouch a lot when things are not "just right"? Do you remember to smile and say THANKS when things are "just right"?

August 13

How would you like to have a "window on the world"? Today would be a good day to make yourself one! Just take a piece of construction paper and cut a tiny little square out of the center of it. Pretend that little square is a window and then draw a house around the window. What kind of house would you like — a farmhouse, a skyscraper, a castle? When you finish drawing and decorating, go to a real window. Close one eye and then hold up the paper "window" close to your face and peep through it with your other eye. Like a telescope, your "window on the world" will help you ZERO IN on one thing at a time — and that's fun. Sometimes all the big things get in the way so you don't notice all the little, special things. How many things can you spot through your window that were made by God?

August 14

It's time for the Name Game again! Did you know Frederick — or Fred — means "peaceful ruler," and Henry means "ruler of a home," while Bridget means "strength," and Constance — or Connie — means "firm and steady one"? Would you like to rule a home or a kingdom? Would you be peaceful, strong, or steady?

August 15

Today's the feast of the Assumption of the Blessed Virgin — the time when Jesus' Mother, Mary, went to join her Son in heaven. Wouldn't this be a great day to give a MERRY surprise to your mother or grandmother or a friend's mother — maybe a little bunch of flowers or a homemade gift or a card or a cookie?

August 16

It's time for Davy Crockett Day! Tomorrow's the birthday of the famous frontiersman who traveled Tennessee, talking and trapping — and hunting bear! His speeches were always full of funny stories, and people liked him and his stories so much they elected him to Congress — and he went from the woods to Washington! Do you like to hear funny stories? Celebrate Davy's Day by making a Family Joke Book! Cut out some funny things from the comic pages of the newspaper and paste them in a scrapbook or notebook. Every time you see a funny cartoon or hear a funny joke, add it to your book. Then when members of your family get gloomy or blue, you can cheer them up with your "Happy Book"!

August 17

Did you ever see a teakettle start to steam? Well, on this day in 1807 people on the riverbank of the Hudson River in New York saw a startling sight — the first steamSHIP! It was built by Robert Fulton and was named "The Clermont." (Up until then there had only been sailing ships or canal boats or rowboats.) Some people even came running with buckets of water, thinking a ship that had smoke coming out of it must be on fire! Put on the teakettle today and have a cup of tea — in honor of Fulton and all the inventors who used the brains God gave them to discover new ways to make life interesting.

August 18

Merry Birthday to Meriwether Lewis, an American pioneer! He was only twenty-nine years old when Thomas Jefferson sent him and William Clark on an expedition to discover what kind of land lay between the Mississippi River at St. Louis and the Pacific Ocean in California. It took the Lewis and Clark expedition a year and a half to travel over the wild and untamed land that only Indians had seen before. Would you be brave enough to explore somewhere you had never been before? That's what you do every time you read a new book or learn a new lesson! Be brave. Learn something new today!

August 19

Did you ever play the game of charades? You take the title of a movie or book and ''act out'' the words silently while other people try to guess it. Well, how about playing Bible charades today? ''Act out'' some of your favorite Bible stories — like Noah and the Ark, Daniel in the Lion's Den, the Good Samaritan, Joseph's Coat of Many Colors. The Bible has so MANY great stories!

August 20

It's the feast of Saint Bernard, who must have been a VERY persuasive fellow. When he decided to become a priest, Bernard talked THIRTY-ONE of his friends and relatives (including four of his brothers) into going with him. They ALL became priests! If YOU wanted to talk someone into becoming a priest, what would you say?

August 21

Yesterday was the birthday of Benjamin Harrison, the twenty-third president of the United States and the third one in his family to make American history! His grandfather, William Henry Harrison, was ALSO a president of the United States. And his great-grandfather was one of the signers of the Declaration of Independence! What a family! Do you know what kind of work your grandfather did — or your great-grandfather? Today ask your folks to tell you about YOUR ancestors. Do you think they had the same kind of dreams and hopes and goals that you do?

August 22

This is a royal day — the feast of the Queenship of Mary! To celebrate Jesus' Mother, Mary, as the Queen of heaven, say a rosary today — or a Hail Mary. Then think about how wonderful it is that all of Jesus' friends will someday be with him in heaven. Are you a friend of Jesus?

August 23

Tomorrow's the feast of one of Jesus' friends, the apostle, Saint Bartholomew. Do you know the names of ALL twelve apostles? Here's a list for you to memorize: Peter, Andrew, James the Greater, James the Less, John, Philip, Thomas, Jude, Matthew, Simon, Bartholomew, and Judas! (Remember that Judas betrayed Jesus and Saint Matthias was chosen to take his place — so you'll want to remember the name of Matthias too!)

August 24

This day in 1814 was a sad one in American history. British soldiers marched on Washington and BURNED the White House and the Capitol! During the battle, President Madison's wife, Dolly, frantically raced about the White House gathering as many of the nation's "historic treasures" as she could pile into her carriage. Finally, at the last possible moment, the president's wife fled, leaving behind all her OWN possessions to burn; but she was glad she had been able to save many things that would be important to future generations of Americans. Within a few years the White House and Capitol were rebuilt, and they looked even more beautiful than before! Thank God today for all the brave men and women in America's history; and ask God to help YOU be a brave American too.

August 25

This is the birthday of the French King Louis VIII, who was such a good king and such a good man he became SAINT Louis! It is also the birthday of a Russian czar who was such a cruel man he became known as Ivan the Terrible! In the world there are a few people who are very, very good, and a few who are very, very bad — and a lot who are usually good but sometimes a little bad. Which are you? Maybe today you could try a little harder to be VERY good!

August 26

Did you know that until August 26, 1920, only MEN could vote in American elections? On this day a new amendment to the Constitution passed; and ever since, women can vote too! The right to vote is one of the special FREEDOMS of America! Suppose you were asked, ''Who is the most special person born in the history of the world?'' Who would you vote for? A movie star? An astronaut? Christopher Columbus? Florence Nightingale? George Washington? Eleanor Roosevelt? Martin Luther King, Jr.? Mother Teresa? Captain Kangaroo? What about Jesus Christ?

August 27

Say hooray for Saint Monica today! This saint had a hot-tempered husband and a trouble-making son! But she never gave up praying for them and hoping they would change. Her son even asked her to *stop* praying for him because he liked being bad! But she didn't stop. Finally, after years of prayer, her patience paid off — her husband was baptized and her son became a priest! Do you ever get impatient and tired of working or waiting for something? Pray today for God to teach you patience.

August 28

Say hooray for Saint Monica's son — who became Saint Augustine! After spending years at odds with the Church, he became a great Church leader, writer, and teacher — one of the most famous in history! Isn't God wonderful to be so forgiving? Even when people turn away from him, God waits patiently; but as soon as they say they're sorry, he welcomes them back with open arms! When you do something wrong, do you always remember to tell God you're sorry?

August 29

Did you know God made an animal named an APE and a fruit named a GRAPE? They're very different, but you might find them both in a tree! An ape likes to climb trees and swing from the branches, and a grape grows on a vine that can "climb" up a tree and wrap itself around the branches! Do you like to climb trees? Tell God thanks today for trees and bees and apes and grapes and girls and pearls and boys and toys!

August 30

Do you think it would be exciting to be a spy, a scout, or a conductor on an "underground railroad"? A lady named Harriet Tubman was all three! She began life as a slave but escaped to become a Union spy and scout during the American Civil War. She was also a "conductor"; but her "railroad" had no trains and was called "underground" because it was a SECRET way to help slaves escape by traveling from one "station" — or safe place — to another. Harriet was nicknamed MOSES because she led over three hundred slaves to safety — like Moses in the Bible led his people out of slavery! Today would be a great day to get out the Bible and read the story of Moses!

August 31

Did you know that when astronauts first tried to shave in space, their "weightless" whiskers floated up to the ceiling? A special razor had to be developed that would draw in the whiskers — like a vacuum cleaner! Do you think your dad would like to shave with a vacuum cleaner? Would you like to brush your teeth with a mop? Or comb your hair with a garden rake? Or write homework with a paintbrush? Today think of all the silly ways you could use things in your house to do things you don't usually do with them! And thank God for giving you imagination and laughter.

September 1

What do you do when you hear a siren — that high, wailing sound that comes from a fire engine or police car or ambulance? Do you stop, look, and listen? Well, suppose — starting today — you do one more thing. That siren sound means somebody is in trouble; so whenever you hear it, say a short, silent prayer and ask God to help that somebody!

September 2

Good morning, glory! Did you know the MORNING GLORY — September's flower — is an early bloomer? It wakes up at dawn! The lovely bell-shaped flowers are pale blue or purple and the leaves look like tiny green hearts. But the GLORY does not like the hot sun, so after its early blossoms welcome the dawn, it goes back to sleep in the afternoon. Are YOU the kind of person who gets up in the morning bright and smiling? Then you're a MORNING glory! If it takes a while for your brain to turn on, you're a "later gator"! Early or late, bloom wherever you are "planted."

September 3

It's sapphires for September! If you were born in this month, your "birthstone" is the sapphire, a very valuable jewel that is a beautiful bright blue and is a symbol for wisdom. Be WISE today. Think of a question about God that you would like answered. Then ask someone to "wise you up" and give you the answer!

September 4

When does a bee gather words instead of honey? When it's a spelling bee! Here's a spelling test for you. How do you spell Christian? That should be easy. You should spell it M-E.

September 5

Did you know that on this day in 1882 America's FIRST Labor Day parade was held in New York, and ten thousand working people marched in it? Ever since, the first Monday in September has been a holiday to honor all "working people." What kind of "labor" would you rather do — run errands or run bases in a ball game; wash dishes or wash a new puppy; dig weeds in the garden or dig into a dish of ice cream? Get to work and make up your own WORKING prayer today — something like this: "Help me to do good work today, Lord, because anybody who shirks work is a jerk!"

September 6

Did you know that only God can make a tree? But you could make a "Family Tree"! Draw a family tree and get your folks to help you fill in as many blanks as you can. Put your name at the top, then your mom's and dad's, then your mom's mom and dad and your dad's mom and dad then your mom's mom's mom and dad and your mom's dad's mom and dad; then your dad's mom's mom and dad and your dad's dad's mom and dad, and so on. Thank God for families.

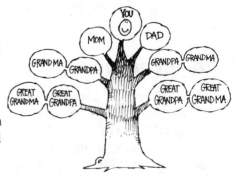

September 7

Did you know that the pretty star-shaped starfish has no teeth but spends most of its time eating? It reaches out with one of its five "arms" and catches an oyster or clam, and then special juices in its stomach digest its dinner! Aren't you glad God gave you teeth to bite into corn on the cob, apples, and peanut brittle — so you don't have to eat just clams and oysters EVERY day! Bite into an apple today and tell God thanks for all the different and interesting ways he made fish, animals, and people!

September 8

Today's the day to celebrate the birthday of Jesus' Mother, Mary. Do it today by giving a surprise UN-birthday present to somebody you know who is named Mary!

September 9

It's the feast of Saint Peter Claver, a missionary who worked for people who were slaves in the West Indies. Peter said he wanted to be "the slave of the slaves," and he truly was. He was their doctor, tending to the sick and wounded and even the lepers. He was their "voice," always going to the authorities to try to get better living conditions for them. And he was their friend. All Christians should be willing to help anyone who needs a friend. Who could you help today?

September 10

Did you ever watch a TV show where the policeman looked for fingerprints to solve the crime? Have YOU ever had your fingerprints taken? Ask your folks if you can get an ink pad and take some family fingerprints today! You'll notice that EVERY ONE is different. Of all the people in all the world, God gave each one a special fingerprint. Nobody else will ever have a fingerprint just like yours. Why? Because you are special to God and there is only ONE you!

September 11

Did you know that when you look out your window you are looking through sand? Strange as it may seem, that clear, see-through glass is made by melting sand, limestone, and soda together in a very hot furnace! Later someone discovered how to add COLOR to make those beautiful stained-glass windows seen in some churches. Think about sand in a sandbox today. Imagine you're running your fingers through the sand, and imagine that sand turning into a church window! Aren't inventions and discoveries wonderful? Would you like to be an inventor someday?

September 12

Are you ready to PLAY BALL? Get out your ball and bat to celebrate the fact that in September of 1845 the Knickerbocker Baseball Club was founded — the FIRST team to play by formal rules. And what did those rules include? Underhand pitching, an "out" on balls caught on the first *bounce,* and victory to the first team to score twenty-one runs! The rules have sure changed since then, haven't they? But ONE rule has not changed — the Golden Rule. That rule says — whether you play ball or not — you should always treat other people the way you'd like them to treat you!

September 13

It's the feast of Saint John Chrysostom, a bishop whose name was not REALLY Chrysostom. He became known by that name because he was a wonderful speaker and the word CHRYSOSTOM means GOLDEN-MOUTHED. Do you know anyone who can make a story sound so exciting you can't stop listening? Your pastor? A teacher? A friend? If you know someone like that, give that person a new nickname today — Chrysostom!

September 14

Can you imagine being trapped on an enemy ship in the middle of a battle? During the War of 1812, a young lawyer went on board a British warship to make arrangements for the release of a prisoner; but while he was there the ship began an attack on America's Fort Henry. All night long the young man paced the deck of the ship while cannon shells screamed around him. On the morning of September 14, 1814, "by dawn's early light," Francis Scott Key could see the stars and stripes of the American flag still flying, and he knew that the enemy had not won. The song he wrote that night is called "The Star-Spangled Banner," and it became America's national anthem. Pray today for all the brave men and women who have defended YOUR flag and YOUR country.

September 15

Today's the feast of Our Lady of Sorrows. Do you know the five Sorrowful Mysteries of the rosary? They are: the Agony in the Garden (when Jesus was praying and his apostles went to sleep); the Scourging at the Pillar (when the Roman soldiers beat Jesus); the Crowning with Thorns; the Carrying of the Cross; and the Crucifixion and Death of Jesus. Pray a rosary today and think about the Sorrowful Mysteries (or events in the life of Jesus). (If you don't know the Joyful and Glorious Mysteries, see September 17 and 20.)

September 16

If you go to an art museum, you may see some paintings by a famous artist known as Tintoretto. He was born on September 16, 1518, and his REAL name was Jacopo Robusti. Do you know why he was called something different? His FATHER worked as a "tintore" — a tinter or dyer — so the son became known as Tintoretto (Little Tintore)! And he was STILL called that even after he became famous! What would YOU be called if you were known by a name connected with your father's work? Would you be known as doctoretto, salesmanetto, accountantetto, plumberetto? Ask God today to bless ALL fathers — AND all sons!

September 17

On September 15 you learned about the Sorrowful Mysteries of the rosary. Now what are the Joyful Mysteries? The Annunciation (when the angel told Mary she would be Jesus' Mother); the Visitation (when Mary went to visit her cousin Elizabeth); the Birth of Jesus; the Presentation in the Temple (when Mary and Joseph took their new baby to be blessed); and the Finding of Jesus in the Temple (after Jesus was "lost"). You can read about all these JOYFUL happenings in the Bible — today!

September 18

During this end-of-summer month, many flowers are still in bloom and many vegetables are being harvested. This would be a good day to play "Look Again"! You've SEEN all these flowers and vegetables before, but did you REALLY look at them? Look at the watermelon. Wasn't that a great idea for God to make a big green thing with a bright pink surprise inside? What would YOU have named it: Greenboat, Pinkheart? Would you have named a carrot an Orange Crunch, an eggplant a Purple Plump, a head of lettuce Mr. Greenleaf? At dinner tonight, rename what you're eating. And thank God for making so many yummies for the tummy!

September 19

M-I-C-K-E-Y M-O-U-S-E! On this day in 1928 the world met Mickey Mouse for the first time! A Disney cartoon called "Steamboat Willie" was shown at the Colony Theater in New York; and from then on Mickey became an American favorite. When you do something silly, people say, "Don't Mickey Mouse around!" But in honor of this anniversary, maybe you SHOULD Mickey Mouse around today: Watch some mouse cartoons while you have a cheese sandwich and thank God for your sense of humor.

September 20

On September 15 and 17 you learned some of the mysteries of the rosary — some of the special happenings in Jesus' life. Today memorize the GLORIOUS MYSTERIES. They are: the Resurrection (when Jesus rose from the dead); the Ascension (when Jesus returned to heaven); the Descent of the Holy Spirit; the Assumption of our Blessed Mother (when Jesus' Mother was taken up into heaven); and the Crowning of Mary as Queen of Heaven. Thank God for glorious happenings.

September 21

It's the feast of Saint Matthew, the tax collector! Did you ever "collect" anything — postage stamps or pretty rocks or marbles or shells or rings or things? In honor of Saint Matthew, start some kind of "collection" today! Find a special box or shelf or corner where you can keep your collection and take it out from time to time to show your friends — because, you know, the very BEST thing you can collect is friends!

September 22

Did you ever see a bug praying? Well, there IS an insect called a PRAYING MANTIS. And you know why? Because it sits back and puts its two front legs together so it LOOKS like people do when they're praying! These bugs like to eat mosquitoes, so people in Japan used to tie a praying mantis to their bedpost at night so IT could have dinner and THEY could sleep without getting mosquito bites! You may think bugs are yucky, but did you know God gave them each an important job to do to keep the environment balanced? Maybe you should take a closer look at bugs. Go out in your yard today and inspect an insect!

OUR FATHER...

September 23

Did you ever hear of a "palindrome"? Here's an example of one: A man, a plan, a canal — Panama. Now look at it BACKWARD. The letters — backward — still spell: A man, a plan, a canal — Panama! A palindrome is a group of words that you can read the same frontward and backward! Could you make up a new palindrome today? Or could you find a new "pal" today? Or could you be a "secret pal" to someone in your family? Leave that person a little present or note or do something to help him or her in some way — secretly, without letting anyone know who did it. God is YOUR "secret pal"; you can't see him, but you know he's with you.

HMMMM...

September 24

Did you know that the seeds of the great redwood tree are so tiny it would take 123,000 of them to weigh ONE pound? Did you ever really see a seed? Did you ever examine one very closely? Some of them are so tiny and wrinkly and ugly — yet one can grow into a beautiful flower and another can grow into a giant redwood tree as tall as a skyscraper! Some days you may feel tiny and unimportant and maybe even ugly too, but if a tiny seed can grow into something special with the help of God's sunshine, you can grow into something special with the help of God's love!

September 25

On this day in 1690 the FIRST newspaper was published in the United States. It was called ***Publick Occurrences***, but it didn't "occur" again because the publisher had failed to get government permission to open his business and the authorities closed it down! Today's newspapers tell you what is happening in your town and your world. But did you ever think about the fact that the Bible tells you what happened in Jesus' world? Think about some Bible story you've heard and rewrite it the way you think it might appear as a news story in today's newspaper!

September 26

It's the feast of Cosmas and Damian, twin brothers who became saints! They were skilled doctors who were known as "the moneyless ones" because they didn't charge people for taking care of them! Would you like to be a doctor someday? Or a nurse? Or a veterinarian? Or a tree surgeon? There are so many special and wonderful careers you can choose from. Pray today that God will help you choose the one that is just right for you!

September 27

Honor Saint Vincent de Paul today on his feast. There was a time, however, when no one wanted to honor him! Even his friends thought he was a grouchy, hard-to-get-along-with person! But, with God's help, he changed. He became concerned about the needs of poor people and turned into a kindhearted, sensitive man who had one main goal — to help others. Today there is a large organization that has one main goal — to help others. It has members all over the world, and it is called the St. Vincent de Paul Society! Are you ever grouchy or hard to get along with? If you are, pray today for God to help you change too!

September 28

In September of 1912, sheet music for W. C. Handy's song "Memphis Blues" went on sale in Memphis, Tennessee. It was the first time "blues music" had ever been published. Did you ever hear blues music? It's a very AMERICAN kind of music — sometimes slow and serious, sometimes loud and "jazzy." Do you feel serious today or jazzy? Sing a song, listen to music on the radio, listen to the birds singing, listen to the wind blowing. Tell God thanks for the MANY kinds of music in the world.

September 29

Do you feel "angelic" today? You should, because it's the feast of Saints Michael, Gabriel, and Raphael — the archangels. The Bible tells about these angels, but it doesn't say what they LOOK like! Would an angel have wings or a sword or a halo or a harp? What do YOU think an angel looks like?

September 30

Happy feast day to Saint Jerome — a man who spent his life trying to know God better. How could YOU get to know God better? Well, how do you get to know a friend better? You go to his or her house and visit, you talk about what you think about things, you try to find out things about each other, you listen to each other. You can do this with God too. You can go to his house — the church — and visit. You can talk to him by praying. You can try to find out about him by reading the Bible or religious books. And you can sit quietly and LISTEN and think. Do that today; sit and listen and give God a chance to talk to you. Maybe you won't hear from him today — but if you don't today, maybe you will tomorrow or the next day or the next day!

October 1

Do you want to do "big things" with your life? Great! Big is important — but little can be too! Today is the feast of Saint Therese, who is known as the "Little Flower" because she lived life in a "little way"! She was always willing to do humble, small things WITHOUT complaining. Ask Saint Therese to help you remember that sometimes you have to learn to do LITTLE things well — before you can learn to do BIG things!

October 2

Did you know a bee is a "fantabulous" flying machine? It can hover like a helicopter and carry twice its weight in freight — while an airplane can carry only one fourth ITS weight. A bee is a "cargo plane" with a tank inside its body to carry nectar and two "baskets" on its hind legs to carry pollen. And what does it use for fuel? A bit of honey! One bit the size of a pinhead can fuel the bee for three quarters of a mile. Take a minute today to tell God "thanks" for making bee-wildering, bee-witching things like the bee — and like YOU!

BZZZZZZZ

October 3

There are only TWO words in the whole English language that use all the vowels — a, e, i, o, u — in their proper order. Do you know what those two words are? They are: FACETIOUS and ABSTEMIOUS. If you eat or drink moderately (never too much or too little), then one of those words would describe you. If you say something funny or witty — especially at the wrong time — then the other word fits you. Look up both words in the dictionary to see which is which! Then make a list of all the words you know that START with vowels and DESCRIBE God. Here are some: amazing, excellent, incomparable, omniscient, ubiquitous. Do you know what all THOSE words mean? If you don't, look *them* up too!

October 4

Today's the feast of Francis of Assisi — the saint who loved all animals and even made friends with the birds! But did you know Saint Francis was the very FIRST one to build a Christmas crib scene? One Christmas Eve, when people came to midnight Mass, they were surprised to see that Francis had built a little scene with statues of Mary and Joseph and the Baby Jesus, and THEN he had brought in some of his friends — REAL animals — and put them in the straw next to Baby Jesus' crib! So the next time you see a Christmas crib, think of Saint Francis and ask the Baby Jesus to remind you to be kind to your pets and gentle with little animals the way Francis was!

October 5

Did you ever hear of a flower named "hop"? Well, that's the funny-named flower for the month of October! It blooms on lovely twining stems that can grow on trellises or up a garden wall — and the stems always twist from the left to the right! The flowers turn into a cone-shaped "fruit" — and those "hops" are used to make beer. What an unusual flower! Do a hop, skip, and jump today, and rejoice in all the unusual flowers God put on the earth for you to discover!

October 6

Did you ever hear of Bruno Hartenfaust? That may sound like an unusual name, but he was a professor and head of a school, and the pope wanted to make him an archbishop — but you know what Bruno said? He wanted to become a hermit instead! He thought a good way to get closer to God would be to go into the mountains where it would be quiet and he could pray a lot. Later some other men came to join him in this peaceful, quiet life of work and prayer. They became known as the Carthusian monks, and he became known as Saint Bruno! To celebrate Saint Bruno's feast today, be a hermit. Find some nice, quiet spot and just sit and think and dream a while.

October 7

The word "rosary" can mean a garden filled with beautiful roses or a special time filled with beautiful prayers. Today is the feast of Our Lady of the Rosary, so honor Mary by praying a rosary — either by yourself or with your family.

October 8

Now what do you guess the "jewel" for October is? It starts with an "O" just like the month does; and it's name is OPAL! This is a lovely, lustrous stone that is flecked with colors so that it changes as you turn it in the light. The opal stands for hope, health, and long life. So if you have an October birthday, your "birthstone" is the opal, and all through your long life you should hope for the best!

October 9

Do you know why Catholics make novenas? NOVENA comes from a Latin word meaning ***nine***. The apostles spent nine days praying between the Ascension (when Jesus left them to go back to heaven) and Pentecost (when the Holy Spirit came to inspire them). So when there's something very important to pray about, prayers are said every day for nine days in a row, asking God for help. And that's a novena! Can you think of something important enough to pray about for nine days?

October 10

Do you know what Ralph Waldo Emerson said about heroes? He said, "A hero is no braver than anyone else; he's only brave five minutes longer!" The saints were heroes because they "hung in there"; no matter how hard the job, they just kept working and praying. So if you get scared sometimes, just ask God to help you hang on and hang in there — and you may be a hero too!

October 11

Did you know there are more ants than any other land animal in the world? God designed an ant so it can carry something twenty-seven times as big as itself! (Could you do that?) Ants can build tunnels that last for years! And these tunnels lead to halls and storage rooms they've built too! Ants are great workers and are always busy. So get busy today, and if somebody says you are "antsy," maybe it will be a compliment!

October 12

In 1492, Columbus sailed the ocean blue! He was off to discover America — but it wasn't easy! Columbus had to put up with bad food, unhappy crews, scary storms, and the worry that the world just might be flat instead of round. And if it WAS flat, he might sail right off the end of it! Today as you remember Christopher Columbus, pray that you too will be brave enough and curious enough to explore new possibilities, seek new horizons, and discover God's world of wonders!

October 13

Today's the feast day of Saint Gerald — a saint who was from a noble family and had the title of "Count of Aurillac." Wouldn't this be a good day to COUNT your blessings? Think of all the good, happy things in your life, all the reasons you have to be thankful. They say it's IMPOSSIBLE to be unhappy AND grateful at the same time. So be grateful and be happy!

October 14

If you ever wish you could get a "second chance," think of Saint Callistus, whose feast is today. He was a Roman slave whose master put him in charge of a bank. But Callistus lost all the bank's money, got scared, and ran away. He was caught and sentenced to severe punishment, but the bank's creditors felt sorry for him and got him released. Then he was arrested for FIGHTING while he was trying to get some of the money back! This time he was sentenced to work in the mines — but again someone got him released. Next he was put in charge of a Christian cemetery in Rome, and there he met and became friends with the pope! And do you know what happened when that pope died? Callistus was elected to be the next pope! From slave to pope — what a life, what a saint!

October 15

Did you know that some DOCTORS are not medical doctors? This special title can also be given to someone who doesn't know anything about medicine — but knows a great deal about some other subject. That's why some great religious leaders have been given the title of "Doctor of the Church." And the first woman to ever receive this title was Saint Teresa of Avila, whose feast is today. Saint Teresa was intelligent AND hardheaded, industrious, AND charming. She worked lots but she also prayed lots. Teresa founded convents and monasteries, traveled all over Spain at a time when most people never traveled beyond their own neighborhoods, and wrote letters and books that are still studied and appreciated today — more than 300 years after her death! Would YOU like to be a doctor when you grow up — a Doctor of the Church?

October 16

It's the feast of Saint Gerard Majella, a saint who always had complete trust in God. When he was only twelve years old, Gerard had to leave school and go to work. He had many hardships in his life, but he always trusted God to take care of him — and God always did. One time when he was working as a houseboy, Gerard accidentally dropped the key to the house down a deep well. This was a big problem, but Saint Gerard thought of a simple solution. He took a statue of the Baby Jesus, tied a rope to it, and dropped it into the well. Then he said a prayer for God to help him. When he pulled the rope back up, the house key was in the hand of the statue! Remember Saint Gerard and always trust in God.

October 17

Saint Ignatius of Antioch was a bishop for forty years, but then the emperor began to persecute Christians, and Ignatius was put into a pit with angry lions and was killed. But before he died, he wrote seven letters that told the people of his day how to live like good Christians. His letters became known as some of the most important writings of early Christianity. Remember the bravery of Saint Ignatius on his feast day and try to live like a good Christian.

October 18

Today's the feast of Saint Luke, who was a physician and also the author of one of the Gospels in the Bible. This would be a good day for you and a friend to find a Bible, look up Saint Luke's Gospel, and see what he has to say!

October 19

Did you ever hear of the Huron Indians? Many years ago — before America had become the United States — there were Huron Indians in Canada who knew nothing about Jesus or Christianity. A Jesuit priest named Isaac Jogues decided he wanted to work among those Indians. He could have stayed in France with his wealthy family and lived comfortably the rest of his life. Instead, he traveled to Canada and lived in wigwams and sat by campfires and taught the Indians and baptized many of them. He loved God enough to want to do his work — even though it was hard. Remember Isaac Jogues on his feast today and ANY day when you have work to do that is hard!

October 20

Do you know what a handicap is? Everybody's different — some people have blond hair, some have black . . . some have blue eyes, some have brown. Some like jelly on peanut butter sandwiches, some don't. And some people are different because they have a handicap — they can't see or hear or walk or talk as well as other people. They're different — not strange or unfriendly — just different, the way somebody tall is different from somebody short. God loves them just like he loves you because ALL people are his children. So if you know somebody with a handicap, offer a helping hand! You might be surprised to find out what a good friend somebody DIFFERENT can be!

October 21

Do you know what the first three words in the Bible are? They are ''In the beginning . . . '' Begin something today. Make a new friend. Read a new book. Start a new hobby. Learn a new prayer!

October 22

Do you think it might have been fun for God ''in the beginning'' when he was making the world? He made all kinds of funny surprises for us, didn't he? Like the giraffe's taaaall neck and the huge elephant's tiny tail and tropical birds with bright orange and purple feathers and a turkey that looks like a bird but some of them can't fly. If YOU had been helping God make the animals, what kind of animals would you have made?

October 23

Did you know a caterpillar has more than 2,000 muscles? No wonder this crawly critter can squiggle in and out and round about! Take time today to try out some of the muscles God gave you! Wiggle your fingers, wiggle your toes, shake your head, and crinkle your nose . . . twist your middle and stretch your top, straighten your legs and give a big hop! How many muscles can you count from your head to your toes? Now can you bend your knees and tell God thanks for giving you all those muscles?

October 24

Today's the feast of a weaver! Saint Anthony Claret was the son of a Spanish weaver and worked as a weaver himself until he decided to become a priest. In his lifetime he preached over 25,000 sermons and wrote 144 books and pamphlets. Is that why they say someone is as busy as a weaver? Or is that ''busy as a beaver''? Or busy as a bee? Oh, well, just get busy — and weave yourself an interesting day today!

October 25

You probably know that Saint Peter was the first pope, but do you know the name of the SECOND pope? His name was Linus! (Do you think he had a friend named Charlie Brown?) Say a prayer today for everybody in the world who is named LINUS!

October 26

Here's a riddle for today: ''Why did the girl take her comb to the dentist? Because it had a broken tooth!'' Do you know any other ridiculous riddles? ''Riddle'' your friends today. Make someone happy! Make yourself happy! Thank God for happy people!

October 27

Do you know what the Beatitudes are? Jesus revealed them in the Sermon on the Mount when he gave Christians a list of problems to be overcome and rewards to be received for being faithful followers of Christ. Can you remember any of them? You'll find the whole list on October 29!

October 28

It's the feast of Saints Simon and Jude. They were two of the original followers of Jesus and helped to spread Christianity. Not a whole lot is known about them, but according to legend they preached together in Persia. And in case you don't know where Persia is, that's because today it's called Iran. What other countries can you think of that have changed their names?

October 29

The Beatitudes are:
1. Blessed are the poor in spirit; the reign of God is theirs.
2. Blessed are the sorrowing; they shall be consoled.
3. Blessed are the lowly; they shall inherit the land.
4. Blessed are they who hunger and thirst for holiness; they shall have their fill.
5. Blessed are they who show mercy; mercy shall be theirs.
6. Blessed are the single-hearted; they shall see God.
7. Blessed are the peacemakers; they shall be called the children of God.
8. Blessed are those persecuted for holiness' sake; the reign of God is theirs.

What do the Beatitudes tell you about life today?

October 30

Here's a different "version" of the Beatitudes. Do you "see yourself" anywhere in this list?

1. Happy are those who need God.
2. Happy are those with self-control.
3. Happy are those who are sorry for sin.
4. Happy are those who hunger and thirst for holiness.
5. Happy are the merciful.
6. Happy are those who live with all their heart.
7. Happy are the peacemakers.
8. Happy are those who suffer for doing what is right.

October 31

Well, ghouls and buoys, this is your day to trick or treat! But do you know why this day is called HALLOWEEN? E'en is short for evening — the evening before a "hallowed" or holy day. Halloween is the shortened version of the hallowed evening before the Feast of All Saints — which is tomorrow. Were you named after a saint? If you were, you might like to look up the life story of your saint and then dress up like your "name saint" to celebrate this hallowed evening!

November 1

It's All Saints' Day. But what IS a saint anyway? The dictionary says a saint is a "holy" person — OR — a person who is VERY kind, patient, charitable, and thoughtful of others. Another definition says a saint is "a friend of God." Today the Church honors ALL the saints — not just the ones whose names are known, but all the people like grandmas and grandpas, aunts, uncles, and friends who have been "holy" enough to get into heaven! Do you think that if you start today to be kind, patient, and thoughtful you could be a saint someday too? Sure, you could!

November 2

Get out your coonskin cap — it's the birthday of Daniel Boone, the famous American frontiersman! Did you know the word "boon" means a present or benefit or blessing? Give yourself a present today! Go out in the yard and look for a "surprise" — a pretty rock, a bird's feather, a flower, a leaf. Even simple things can sometimes be great blessings or "treasures"!

November 3

Today's the feast of Saint Martin de Porres — a saint who had lots of jobs. He learned how to be a barber, how to concoct medicines, patch up wounds, and patch up the other monks' robes. But he was especially known for his ability to search through the city and find whatever was needed each day to help the poor — blankets or bandages, candles or cabbages, milk or money. Search through YOUR things today — through your closet or toy box — and see if you can find some things you could give away to help the poor.

November 4

It's the birthday of a famous American named Will Rogers, who once said, "I never met a man I didn't like." Is there anyone you DON'T like? If there is, say a prayer for that person today!

November 5

Did you know the first submarine ever used in a battle — in 1776 — was named the "American Turtle"? Would you like to live in a submarine? Would you like to live in a shell like a turtle and "carry your house with you" wherever you go? Or would you rather live where you do right now? Remember today that no matter where you roam, there's no place as snug as home!

November 6

Saint Leonard, whose feast is today, once received a very unusual reward. The king had asked Leonard to pray for him and — in return — he wanted to do something for Leonard. So the king told Leonard to get on his donkey and ride around for one whole day, and he would be rewarded with all the land he and his donkey had ridden on that day! Give yourself a reward today! You've been busy praying for other people, so today ask someone else to say a prayer for you!

November 7

Today's the birthday of the most famous woman scientist in history! Her name was Marie Sklodowska until she married another great scientist, Pierre Curie, and became known as Madame Curie. She and her husband worked together in the laboratory and in 1903 received the Nobel Prize in physics for their work on radioactivity. After her husband's death, Madame Curie continued their work and in 1911 became the first person to ever receive a SECOND Nobel Prize — for her discovery of radium! Would you like to work in a laboratory someday? Do you realize God made the whole world a "laboratory" — full of wonders for you to discover?

November 8

You don't have to "keep mum" about this — you can tell anyone who wants to know that the flower for November is the chrysanthemum! It's an especially nice flower because it blooms at THE END of summer. Just when most of the other flowers have begun to wilt and go to sleep for the winter, the chrysanthemum pops out in bright blooms to cheer up the world. At the END of today — or any day — when your family is tired and beginning to "wilt," why don't you pop up and offer to help with supper or with the dishes, just like a cheery chrysanthemum!

November 9

November's "jewel" comes in several colors, but it is usually a warm, golden brown — just right for this harvest time of year. If you were born in November, your "birthstone" is the topaz. In honor of the topaz, this would be a good day to toe the line, toe the mark, wear a toga, tap a toe dance, and do as you are told!

November 10

It's the feast of Saint Leo the Great — a great pope who was known for preaching great sermons or homilies. When you hear a homily at Mass on Sunday, do you remember what the priest said? Why don't you ask your family to have a "homily hunt" every Sunday? Challenge each one to remember one thing from the homily! After Mass, when you're all together — having breakfast, lunch, or dinner — each one can tell the results of the hunt! You could even vote on who has the best memory each Sunday!

November 11

Saint Martin of Tours, whose feast is today, was a pagan and a soldier in the army. But one night he saw a poor beggar freezing in the cold and felt sorry for him, so Martin took his sword and cut his own cloak in half and gave half to the beggar. Later that night Martin dreamed that he saw Jesus — and Jesus was wearing the half of his cloak which he had given the beggar! After that, Martin became a Christian and then a monk and finally a saint. Never be embarrassed to ''feel sorry'' for someone. Whenever you reach out to help, you reach out to Jesus.

November 12

Check your ''schedule'' to see whether you have time to celebrate the birthday of an artist named Rodin — who already lived by a schedule when he was only fourteen years old! Every morning at six o'clock he went to the park to sketch the animals there. At eight o'clock it was time for school. At noon he ate a sandwich lunch while he walked to an art museum to study the paintings there. Then, in the afternoon he worked in a shop to earn money. And at night? More art-work until time to go to bed. But his hard work paid off and he became a famous sculptor. One of his best-known masterpieces is called ''The Thinker.'' And what do you think about that? Maybe you won't become famous, but you can work hard to use the talents God gave you. Which of your talents will you use today?

November 13

Today's the feast of the first United States citizen to be canonized a saint — Mother Frances Xavier Cabrini. She was born in Italy and wanted to be a teacher and a nun and a missionary. For a long time she wasn't able to do any of those things, but finally she came to America to work with the many Italian immigrants who lived in New York and Chicago, where her work was very successful. During her life she opened more than fifty successful schools, orphanages, convents, and hospitals. Do you ever get discouraged because you want to do something but can't? Remember Mother Cabrini today and keep trying!

November 14

Did you ever read the thrilling adventure book *Treasure Island* or the delightful poems in *A Child's Garden of Verses*? Well, today's the birthday of the man who wrote those books — Robert Louis Stevenson. Would you like to write a book someday? Well, why not start today? Write about all the special things God gives you in November — trees with colored leaves, warm days with a cool breeze, and a Happy Thanksgiving time, if you please!

November 15

One of the FIRST and greatest scientists was also a saint — Saint Albert the Great, whose feast is celebrated on this date. Albert was interested in everything, so he decided to write a huge book about many of his interests — science, mathematics, language, logic, metaphysics, politics, and astronomy. It took him twenty years to complete the book! Would YOU have the patience to work on ONE project for twenty years? Pray today for patience and perseverance!

November 16

A make-believe character named Phineas Fogg traveled *Around the World in 80 Days* in a book written by Jules Verne. In November of 1889 a woman newspaper reporter decided she would try to BEAT that record! People couldn't wait to get the newspaper each day to see where her travels had taken her, but when she returned — in only seventy-two days — women were shocked to learn that she had traveled WITHOUT AN UMBRELLA! At that time ''proper'' ladies ALWAYS took along an umbrella! You don't need an umbrella — even on rainy days — when you travel in your imagination. Close your eyes today and pretend you are discovering all the wonders God has put in other parts of the world.

November 17

Did you know there are 15,000 different kinds of rice? If God made that many kinds of rice, imagine how many different kinds of people he made! Look at all the people you see today. Each one has a face with two eyes, a nose, a mouth, and two ears — but each face looks so different from every other face! Isn't it wonderful that God's creations are so endlessly interesting?

November 18

Did you ever have a wintertime picnic? No matter what the weather's doing today — snowing, blowing, freezing, or breezing — ask your folks if you can have a picnic IN THE LIVING ROOM! Just move back the furniture, spread a picnic cloth, sit on the floor, use paper plates and napkins, and have a sandwich supper. Sing songs or tell jokes and "have a picnic" of a good time. Then thank God for no picnic ants!

November 19

Did you ever hear Abraham Lincoln's "Gettysburg Address" that starts "Fourscore and seven years ago . . . "? On November 19, 1863, people gathered to hear a famous "orator" give a TWO-HOUR SPEECH! When he had finished, the audience realized President Lincoln spoke for less than two minutes. No one remembers what the other man said that day, but Americans will never forget what Lincoln said. He said that America will always have "government of the people, by the people, and for the people." Say a prayer of thanks today for living in the land of the people.

UM...EXCUSE ME. WHAT'S YOUR ADDRESS?

November 20

How about an ABC day today? Make a scrapbook and on the front print "God is. . . . " On the inside print all the letters of the alphabet and then try to think of a word that starts with each letter to describe God. God is . . . A, all-knowing; B, boundless; C, caring; D, dependable; E, everywhere. . . . If you can't think of a word for each letter, ask your family or friends to help.

November 21

On the fourth Thursday of November, the United States celebrates harvest time with a Thanksgiving holiday. This tradition began with the Pilgrims and the Indians, but it finally became a national holiday in 1863 — thanks to a lady named Sarah J. Hale. For almost forty years — first as the editor of the *Ladies' Magazine* in Boston and then as editor of *Godey's Lady's Book* in Philadelphia — she kept writing editorials urging that a special date should be set aside when the WHOLE COUNTRY would give thanks for the blessings of the year. At last President Lincoln issued a national Thanksgiving Proclamation, this holiday has been celebrated ever since. What will you be especially thankful for this Thanksgiving?

November 22

In this Thanksgiving time of year, your family might like to make up a special "blessing" to say before each meal. OR you might want to memorize this one: "Bless us, O Lord, and the gifts which we are about to receive, from your goodness, through Christ our Lord. Amen."

November 23

Saint Clement, whose feast is today, is the "patron" of hat makers! Why? Well, there is a legend that Saint Clement once went on a pilgrimage and walked for many miles. To ease his aching feet, he put wool in his sandals. After walking on it, the wool became compressed and turned into a new kind of fabric. This fabric became known as "felt" and was used in making men's and ladies' hats! Put on your hat today and say a prayer of thanks for interesting legends and interesting saints!

November 24

Did you ever say a "beanbag" prayer? Ask your family — or some friends — to stand in a circle and toss a beanbag today. Whoever catches the beanbag should say a prayer — a thanksgiving prayer for this special time of year. What prayer will YOU say? Thank you, God, for pumpkin pie. . . . Thank you, God, for puppy dogs. . . . Thank you, God, for. . . .

November 25

Today's the birthday of Andrew Carnegie, a poor boy who started out working in a factory but became one of the wealthiest men in America. He believed money should be used for the public good and donated about 350 million dollars to be used for education and other philanthropies. Some of his money was used to open 2,800 libraries across the country! Visit a library today and thank God for people who help other people.

November 26

Did you know bees have air conditioning in their homes? When the weather gets hot enough to threaten to melt the wax in their hive, a group of bees goes to the hive entrance and another group stays inside. Then both groups begin to flap their wings — at a rate of four hundred flaps per second! This creates a cross-draft that pulls out the hot air and brings in cooler air! Isn't that a cool idea? Have a peanut butter and honey sandwich today and thank God for making smart bees — and smart boys and girls.

November 27

Did you ever play "Show and Tell"? Get some of your friends together today and play Bible "Show and Tell" "Show" something that illustrates a Bible story — and then make everybody guess which story it is. For example, "show" an apple for the story of Adam and Eve, a slingshot for David and Goliath, and two glasses of tomato juice for the parting of the Red Sea!

UMMM

November 28

A wise man once said that the world is like a mirror. Frown at it and it will frown back, at you. Smile at it and it will smile back, and you will have a happy life. When you look at the world today, will it be with a frown or a smile?

November 29

Did you ever read the book *Little Women*? It has been a very popular book with girls and boys for many years — and it was written by Louisa May Alcott, whose birthday is today. Say a prayer today for all the heroic women of our world.

November 30

Did you ever read the book ***Tom Sawyer***? It has been a very popular book with boys and girls for many years; it was written by Mark Twain, whose birthday is today. In that book Tom tried to trick his friends into helping him "whitewash" or put white paint on a fence. Do you ever try to "whitewash" your faults — pretending that every mistake you make is really somebody else's fault? Ask God to forgive you for all the times you've put the blame on somebody else when you were really the one at fault.

December 1

Here's the month to be advent-urous! Why? Because it's the time of Advent — a word which means "coming" or "waiting." It's the time of waiting for Jesus' birthday to come! "Adventure" today deep into your brain and think about this: What present can you give Jesus for Christmas? He doesn't need candy or crayons, a football or a footstool. But you SHOULD have a gift for him, since Christmas IS his birthday. What gift will it be?

December 2

Do you have an Advent calendar? Use it — or any calendar — to start the Christmas countdown. Each morning check off the date and count how many days are left until Christmas. How many days do you have left to get that present for Jesus? If you're still wondering what gift you could give, here are some suggestions: Do someone else's chores every day for a week *plus* your own . . . say a rosary each day for a week . . . do something you don't like to do *without* complaining . . . say this little extra prayer every day until Christmas: "Dear Jesus, I love you and thank you for coming into the world on Christmas — to save me and to be my friend."

December 3

It's the feast of Saint Francis Xavier, one of the GREATEST Christian missionaries, a man who happily shared his life with the poorest of the poor and brought the Good News of Jesus to thousands of people in the East Indies and the Orient. Get out a globe or map today and see if you can find any of these places: Cape Comorin, Sri Lanka, New Guinea, the Philippines, Japan. Do you think you might travel to those places someday? If you do, you'll sail the seas and walk the land where Saint Francis bravely journeyed to bring the teachings of Christianity to people who had never heard of Jesus before!

December 4

Did you know each week of Advent has a "theme" or idea to think about? The first week it's EXPECTATION. EXpectation can be EXciting — when you're waiting for your birthday party to begin! It can also be EXasperating — when you're waiting for a school bus that's late or for dinner to be ready when you're hungry. What do you EXPECT Christmas to be like this year? What could YOU do to make it a happier time for someone else?

December 5

Can you guess the name of the flower for the month of December? Ho, ho, ho! It's holly! With bright green leaves and bright red berries, what could be better than holly for the holidays? The name holly actually means "holy tree," so maybe today would be a good day to climb a tree and say a prayer! Or do something tree-mendously holy!

December 6

It's Saint Nicholas Day. Did you put your shoes out last night? In some countries it's the custom for children to leave their shoes at the door on the night before Saint Nicholas Day; and when they wake up the next morning they find a shoeful of candy! Here's a fun idea for a family game tonight — a shoe swap! Ask everybody to wear somebody else's shoes during dinner! Pretend you are the person whose shoes you are wearing; and think how it must feel to be that person! What makes that person happy or sad, worried or glad, disappointed or excited? Getting to know someone better makes it easier to love someone better!

December 7

It's the feast of Saint Ambrose, a bishop who was exactly what people thought a bishop SHOULD be — holy, scholarly, patient, and courageous in defending Church teachings. Send a Christmas card to your bishop today. Won't he be surprised!

December 8

It's a holy day — the Feast of the Immaculate Conception of the Blessed Virgin Mary! In some countries this day is celebrated as Mother's Day, and all the children dress in their First Communion clothes to march in a procession honoring Jesus' Mother, Mary. Why don't you write a "Mother's Day" letter to your mother — and tell her how much you love and honor her!

December 9

It's time to think about the "theme" for the second week of Advent — JOY! Think today of all the joy in this month: the joy of planning for the holy day of Christmas, the joy of sharing with others by giving them gifts, and especially the joy of knowing that Jesus gave himself as a gift to the world on that first Christmas!

December 10

It's a dynamite day — time to remember the man who invented dynamite! Alfred Nobel made a lot of money from his invention, and then he did something even more explosive! He said he wanted to use his money to give PRIZES to people who did something special for the world. On this day in 1910 the FIRST Nobel prizes were given, and they are now awarded every year to those who achieve something "significant" in the fields of medicine, chemistry, physics, literature, or working for the cause of peace. If you could give a prize to someone you think made the world better, who would get your prize? Think about that today.

December 11

Do you know what the forecast is for tonight? Dark! Do you know what the forecast is for next Tuesday night? Dark! Yep, all nights are dark — but that's OK. Dark can be mysterious and fun. Dark brings the sight of the stars and the light of the moon! Dark gives the earth a chance to rest and dream. When you say your prayers tonight, thank God for the dark and the light, the night and the day, the now and the someday. And dream happy dreams. Tomorrow will be one day closer to Christmas.

December 12

It's the Feast of Our Lady of Guadalupe — another special day to honor Mary, a feast celebrated especially in Mexico with prayers and processions. This would be a good day to get out your family's Christmas crib set — Mary, Joseph, the Baby Jesus, the shepherds, and lambs. If you don't have a crib set, buy one or make one! Just draw the Christmas scene on construction paper or cardboard. Put your crib scene in a special place of honor in your home as a reminder that it will soon be Happy Birthday, Jesus Day!

December 13

Did you know the month of December got its name from the Latin word for ''ten'' because it was once the tenth month of the year instead of the twelfth? If you were going to name this month of snow and jingle bells and Santa Claus and holly and mistletoe and Jesus' birthday, what would you name it? Snowary? Jinglember? Hollydays? Christmonth?

December 14

Did you know that the first jewelry described in history belonged to a queen of Egypt and was made of gold and turquoise? The bright blue-green turquoise is the "jewel" for this month. So if you were born in December, your "birthstone" is historic as well as beautiful! What else can you think of that is historic as well as beautiful? The White House . . . your parish church . . . your grandmother? Make history today. Do something "beautiful" for someone in your family!

December 15

Did you ever hear of Boxing Day? No, it's not a day to reach out and punch someone. In England and Canada it's the day people give boxes of gifts to workers who serve in a special way — for example, those who deliver the mail, drive the school bus, pick up the garbage, work in a shop. Is there someone you would like to honor with a surprise box? What about your pastor or the school nurse or a Scout leader or a room mother? Ask your folks if you can start now to make or buy some little gifts to box — cookies or candies, a fancy loaf of bread, a puzzle or paperweight, or any kind of little gift you think would be just right to say "Thanks!"

December 16

Do you know what the third theme for Advent is? It's HOPE. Think about that today. What is hope? Well, it's like a little electric light inside your head that keeps brightening your view of the world, telling you that things are good now and will get even better! Hope is like the purr of a kitty cat or the warmth of a soft sweater that makes you feel cozy and tells you everything will be all right. Hope is God.

December 17

Soar, explore. Fly high, look at the sky, and say "Hi." On this day in 1903 at Kill Devil Hill, North Carolina, near the village of Kitty Hawk, the Wright brothers PROVED that man can fly! The first successful flight in their homemade airplane was made by Orville Wright and lasted only twelve seconds! The next flight — by brother Wilbur — lasted fifty-nine seconds. That was still less than a minute, but it was more flying than anyone else had ever done before! God didn't give people wings, but he did give them imagination. Use yours today.

December 18

Did you know God made an animal named an *antelope* and a fruit named a *cantaloupe!* They may sound a lot alike, but they really are quite different. Though a cantaloupe is a melon and an antelope could be melon-choly, you can't have an antelope for breakfast or take a ride on a cantaloupe. Didn't God make a lot of fun things? Thank him today for antelopes and cantaloupes, tomatoes and potatoes, dogs and frogs, rhymes and Christmastimes!

December 19

Are you going to ''cark'' today or be ''corking''? Well, you don't want to ''cark'' because that means to worry or be troubled. But ''corking'' means to be extremely terrific. So don't cark about Christmas. Pray about it! Ask God to help your family have the most blessed — and most ''corking'' — Christmas ever!

December 20

Do you know what the fourth theme for Advent is? It's ACCEPTANCE. Remember when an angel came and told Mary that God would like her to be the Mother of Jesus? Mary didn't say, ''I can't talk to you now — wait until the commercial.'' Mary didn't say, ''Maybe I will — but why do I have to?'' Mary just said ''yes.'' She accepted the job she was given. She was ready to do whatever God wanted her to do. Do you ever say, ''Why?'' ''Wait a minute'' . . . ''Maybe''? Are you ready to accept whatever job God wants you to do?

December 21

It's time for a rock concert! Did you know it was on this day in 1620 that the Pilgrims landed at Plymouth Rock? To celebrate that long voyage of the founding fathers, go out in the yard today and pick up some rocks! There may not be any flowers blooming in your yard at this time of the year, but you should be able to find plenty of rocks! Did you ever notice that even rocks can be special? Some have ''layers'' . . . some are smooth, some jagged . . . some are speckled with colors, some have interesting shapes. Consider today how wonderful it is that God could even make a rock pretty! And here's a last-minute Christmas gift idea — clean up a rock and then use magic markers to draw on a design or ''happy face'' and give it to someone to use as a ''Merry Christmas'' paperweight!

December 22

Did you know millions of trees in the world are planted by forgetful squirrels? The squirrels bury nuts to hide them away for the winter — then forget where they hid them! In the spring the nuts sprout and eventually grow into tall trees. Do something nutty today. Put a dish of nuts in your backyard — a Christmas treat for those forgetful squirrels!

December 23

Here's a Christmas tongue twister for you: "Captain Christopher cooked a crumbly cake for Christmas. If Captain Christopher cooked a crumbly cake for Christmas, where's the crumbly Christmas cake Captain Christopher cooked?" Christmas is a busy and exciting time, and sometimes busy people get their tongues twisted and say something naughty, not nice! Don't let that happen to you! (But if it ever does, be sure to say you're sorry!)

December 24

The stockings are hung. The presents are wrapped. The tree is decorated! Ohhh . . . it's so exciting! Ask your family if you can gather around the Christmas tree tonight before you go to bed and say a little Christmas prayer. Maybe you'd like to use this one: "Dear God, bless this tree and those who gather around it. Thank you for the green of the tree that reminds us of the ever-green, never-dying love you give us. Thank you for the lights to remind us that Jesus is the Light of the world. Thank you for the decorations to remind us of all the wonderful things you've given us to decorate our lives. Bless our family — in the name of the Father and of the Son and of the Holy Spirit. Amen.''

December 25

It's here at last! Merry, happy, blessed Christmas! Suggest to your family that at dinnertime you all join hands and sing "Happy birthday, dear Jesus, happy birthday to you!''

December 26

When you woke up this morning, did you remember to say "Good morning, God"? A good way to start any day is with a little hello prayer. Here's one you might like to memorize today: "Dear God, I offer you today all my prayers, works, joys, and sufferings. Help me today to know you and love you and serve you. Amen."

December 27

Today's the feast of the youngest apostle, Saint John. He was one of Jesus' special friends and the only apostle who was with Jesus at the Crucifixion. Sometimes when you are young, you don't feel very important or powerful — but you are! You have the power to make someone else smile or feel happy or feel loved. Use your important power today.

December 28

Today's a sad feast day — the Feast of the Holy Innocents. Do you know the Bible story about King Herod? Herod heard that the Baby Jesus was going to be a king, and he didn't want another king threatening him, so he decided to have Baby Jesus killed! But he didn't know where to find Baby Jesus — so he sent his soldiers into Bethlehem and told them to kill all the babies under two years of age. An angel had warned Joseph to take Jesus and Mary on a journey into Egypt, so they were gone before the soldiers came; but all the other innocent babies were killed. Say a prayer for all the innocent babies who are being killed by abortion in the world today.

December 29

Did you know that the last Sunday in December is usually celebrated as the Feast of the Holy Family? Get out the Christmas cards you received this year and look for pictures of the Holy Family — Jesus, Mary, and Joseph. How many different pictures can you find? Do you think the Holy Family was anything like your family? Ask God to help your family be a stronger, closer family next year — and try to think of something you could do to help make it that way!

December 30

Did you know that a curl is a twisty curve in your hair . . . that curling is a game where you slide a stone along the ice . . . that a curlicue is a fancy squiggle you add when you're writing something . . . and that a curlew is a large brown bird with skinny legs and a long beak that turns downward? Add a "twist" to today — play a game, write a Christmas "thank you" note and put some curlicues on it — but don't turn your beak down. Turn it up and smile!

December 31

It's the last day of the old year — and time to think about a brand-new year! Did you know that if there's a half glass of milk on the table, a "pessimist" looks at it and says the glass if half empty; but an "optimist" looks at it and says it's half full. Which are you? Do you see the good or the bad? Do you see this day as an end or as a beginning? Pray today for God to fill you with all four "themes" of Advent — expectation, joy, hope, and acceptance — and you'll begin to have a very Happy New Year!